new
STREAMSIDE
GUIDE

to naturals and their imitations

ART FLICK'S
new
STREAMSIDE
GUIDE

to naturals and their imitations

Introduction by
RAYMOND R. CAMP

illustrated in color and halftone

CROWN PUBLISHERS, INC., NEW YORK

ACKNOWLEDGMENTS

I wish to express my gratitude to Dr. Herman T. Spieth for identifying the May flies collected; to Preston Jennings for starting me off "on the right foot"; to Raymond R. Camp, who by his constant prodding finally got me to do this book; to the many fisherman friends who helped me try out the "experimental" flies and nymphs; and to Willis Stauffer, for having started me on that most enjoyable of pastimes, fly-tying.

For this new edition, I am grateful to the late Leslie Thompson for standing permission to use his excellent drawings of May flies and nymphs. My very special thanks go to Doug Swisher and Carl Richards for allowing me to include some of the superb color photographs from their book *Selective Trout*.

© *1969 by Arthur B. Flick*

LIBRARY OF CONGRESS CATALOG CARD
NUMBER: 70–95614
ISBN: 0-517-507838
PRINTED IN THE UNITED STATES OF AMERICA

Published simultaneously in Canada by General Publishing Company Limited Ninth Printing, August, 1973

TO MY WIFE, LITA,
WHOSE PATIENCE WITH ME
EVEN EXCEEDS MINE WITH TROUT.
NOW, AFTER FORTY-FIVE YEARS, I STILL
HAVE NOT EXHAUSTED HER PATIENCE.

Color photographs by
DOUG SWISHER *and* CARL RICHARDS

Drawings by Leslie P. Thompson.

CONTENTS

CONTENTS

PREFACE TO THE NEW EDITION

NEEDLESS TO SAY, I'm delighted that STREAMSIDE GUIDE is being reissued. During the years it was out of print I received scores of requests for copies, so I hope those I had to turn down are as pleased as I that it is again available.

I found I could make a few changes, most of a minor nature, which I hope will cause readers a bit less confusion in attempting to identify the naturals. One important fly has been added, *Ephemerella attenuata* (Blue-winged Olive), which was left out of the other edition due to our inability to get it identified. Also, the expanded

chapter on nymphs and the new one on summer
and autumn angling should add to the book. Without doubt, the most important additions are the
superb photographs of the naturals by Doug
Swisher (whom I was able in a small way to assist
in collecting), along with the late Let Thompson's
drawings of nymphs and flies drawn from life.

Though I was naturally pleased with all the
mail that came in when the book was first published, and which has continued up to right now,
a lot of people asked me to supply them with the
patterns mentioned in the book; I had to tell them
politely, and want to restate it here, that I am *not*
a commercial fly-tyer.

As the NEW STREAMSIDE GUIDE goes to
press, I'd like to think a bit into the future. Easy
access and much more free time has of course put
a lot more pressure on our streams and rivers. So
have many of the needs of our modern world:
faster roads, the need for more water, and so
forth. The no-kill and trophy-fish-only sections
set aside on some streams are a great help and I
feel that our right-thinking conservation depart-
ments will expand them as soon as the general
public realizes they are a good thing for trout fishing; our conservation people are really trying to
do a good job—when the so-called sportsmen will
let them; and groups like Trout Unlimited are
invaluable.

But there's also work for each of us, each

time we wade our favorite river. As you teach
your children and friends about the habits of trout
and how to catch them, also teach them how to
protect their streams, especially the tributaries.
Just as a forward cast cannot be better than a back
cast, a main stream can be no better than its
feeders. In these smaller streams get them to plant
a few willow shoots, for instance, each time they
fish them. And do it yourself, for willows will work
wonders in stream rehabilitation. On a small local
stream where one of my boys and I fished, we did
this each time out and the work was continued on
a much larger scale by employees of the Stream
Improvement unit of our Bureau of Fish. This,
along with some well-placed dams and deflectors,
has improved the physical condition of this stream
to such an extent that it is hard to believe it is the
same body of water. Take it from one who "lives"
trout fishing—this type work is invaluable for our
future fishing and is so much more important than
stocking that there is simply no comparison. The
banks are now contained; the stream bed is nar-
rower and deeper; fly life, so necessary, has increased unbelievably; and, most important, with
a better stream in which to live, trout are far more
numerous than in the past. Of greater importance
is the increase in natural reproduction, furnishing
us with more *wild* fish, at *no cost to anyone*.

Except where the road builders or reservoir
people have been especially unthinking, the aquat-

ic insects of greatest importance to trout fishermen, the May flies, come back each year with the regularity of a great natural law. Let's protect our streams so *they'll* come back each year as well, for our children and grandchildren.

And teach your children to fly fish early in their stream careers. One of my grandsons, a ten-year-old, is going to get his first lesson this year and I hope it will mean he will take his first trout on a dry fly at that tender age. It's a thrill I look forward with great anticipation to sharing.

I sincerely hope this little guide will someday help him—and your grandchildren too.

ART FLICK

INTRODUCTION

by
RAYMOND R. CAMP

MANY YEARS AGO I stood hip-deep in a stream and contemplated (with a pride that would be considered justifiable only by another fisherman) the first trout I had ever taken on a dry fly tied by myself. An hour ago I turned the final page in the manuscript of this book. As I did so I became aware of a feeling of pride that will be understood by every angler who reads these pages. I was proud of the very small part I had played in making it possible for the fly fishermen of this country to possess this book.

Art Flick did not want to write a book. I wanted him to write this one. For every argument he advanced against the project I had two in favor of it. His contention that there were "too many books on trout fishing" was one of the easiest to refute. I pointed out that there was not one on the subject in question. Then came the plaint that the additional research required with the impedimenta of the entomologist would rob him of hours that could be spent on the stream with a rod. Against this logic, I could not argue.

Mine was an uphill task, but at last I realized I had won. On a bright May day on the Schoharie I found Art within splashing range of a trout, with a collecting vial instead of a rod in his hand. Only one familiar both with the Schoharie and Art's love of this stream can appreciate what he sacrificed in order to complete his research on May flies and the trout that feed upon them. Which of us would have the temerity to raise a scornful finger if occasionally the temptation to fish was too great?

I have known Art Flick for many years, and I had fished with him only a short time when I realized a great respect for his knowledge of flies and streamcraft. This was not unmixed with an envy of his proximity to a stream where this craft could be so happily practiced.

Once he had agreed to tackle the book, I knew the result would be a thorough job, for every fly he tied was flawless, every cast he made was studied. But I did not know the result would attain the stature of this volume.

A long time ago, even as anglers measure time, a man began the greatest of all volumes on fishing with the observation that he could not hope to "make a man that was none, an angler by a book." This book, likewise, contains no magic formula for the overnight transformation of a novice into an experienced angler. But I know of no fly fisherman, and I meet thousands every year, who would not be richly rewarded by reading these pages.

I have learned, through experience not untinged with bitterness, that the writer on angling matters who dares the *absolute* is inviting both censure and a mountain of mail. On this one occasion, however, I am conscious of no foreboding when I state: this volume is of more real value to the fly fisherman than any book I have ever read. Of all the books on trout fishing, and I have waded through a legion of them, this is the one about which I can say: "I wish I had written that." I can think of no other for which I would trade a dozen of Art Flick's dry flies.

Few trout fishermen have either the time or the inclination to make a real study of the flies that play such an important part in their fishing. An even lesser number study the habits, habitat, and life cycles of the natural flies that serve as a pattern for the artificials, and still fewer attempt to discover when, why, and how the trout feed on these flies.

Now, it is not necessary to concern yourself with these matters—Art Flick has done it for you.

Walton once pointed out that "no man is born an artist or an angler." Whether the ultimate is a fine landscape or a memorable day on the stream, guidance, study, and practice are essential. A great wealth of guidance is contained in these pages. The rest is up to you.

If this small volume does not accompany you on every trip to the stream, you are a lukewarm angler indeed, and would do well to forsake fly fishing for a duller pastime.

EXPLANATORY NOTE

"WHAT FLY shall I use?"

Probably no question equals this one in importance so far as the average trout fisherman is concerned, and to the dry-fly angler it has an even greater significance. The first concern of the fly fisherman, once he has mastered the mechanics of casting, is the use of the right fly at the right time.

Could I answer that question with a degree of accuracy that would guarantee success on every occasion, I would decline as gracefully but as firmly as possible. The angler possessed of such knowledge would have the golden eggs without the suspense of keeping the goose alive. Were it possible to take a limit of trout every time we fished our favorite stream, how long would it take before the sport began to pall? Fortunately, the anticipation is still greater than the realization, and God grant this may always be.

Fly fishermen are concerned primarily with the task of correlating the artificial and the natural fly. If, in these pages, they find enlightenment on this important subject, the purpose of the book will have been attained.

I do not expect the rank and file of commercial fly-tyers to agree with everything that follows. They may feel that some of my findings would affect their business, for I do not recognize the value of many of the commercial fly patterns. However, I want to make it clear that the artificials I discuss later are not the *only* effective flies, but merely those that bring the best results when certain May flies are on the stream. The better fly-tyers will realize they have more to gain than to lose in a reduction of the number of patterns, for they know that many of those now tied could very easily be eliminated.

It is doubtful that any fly pattern exists that, under some conditions, will not take trout. There are rare occasions when a fish will rise to any fly that floats over him. But this, as we all know, is the exception rather than the rule. Owing to the fact that many anglers are incapable of selecting the correct artificial to match the natural, they carry three times the number of patterns actually required.

All of us have heard it said that a certain pattern is a killer on one stream but valueless on another. This may be true of flies that are not correctly patterned after one of the May flies of importance, but experience has convinced me that a good imitation of any of the naturals discussed herein will prove equally effective on all streams where such naturals exist. It is true that not every species of May fly will be found in every stream, because of the variable characteristics of streams, but most of the species important to the fly fisherman will be found in nearly all trout streams.

I believe it should be mentioned here that my experiments were all conducted on heavily fished waters that were open to public fishing. I have always held that experiments of this nature are valueless if carried out on heavily stocked, lightly fished streams. Most private waters are abundantly stocked with large fish. This brings about increased competition among trout for the available food supply, whereas in public water there is generally more food than is required by the comparatively few fish.

In conclusion, let me explain that the purpose of this book is to help the angler who is dissatisfied with the results he is now getting, and to help him realize his desire to know more about insects that govern his success. I have sought to aid him in identifying the important May flies and the artificial dry flies, and in some instances the nymphs, that imitate them. It is my conviction that the dry-fly enthusiast who can recognize such flies and select their artificial counterparts will take more and better fish, and will no longer find it necessary to ask: "What fly shall I use?"

new
STREAMSIDE
GUIDE

to naturals and their imitations

1

THE SELECTIVITY OF TROUT

IN MOST CASES when fish are feeding on a certain species of May fly, or during the period of what we call a "hatch," they are more selective than at other times.

It is then that it will be to the fly fisherman's advantage to know what fly is on the water, as well as its proper representation. With no more study than it takes to learn to differentiate between the various artificials that most fishermen recognize, the important species of May flies can be identified.

Obviously, when you see fish rising to a certain fly, and know exactly what it is, as well as the correct imitation, you will take more and larger trout.

Some writers maintain that fish are less selective when there is a hatch of flies on the water, and that often in such cases they will take almost any fly of a size that corresponds to the natural.

This may be true on certain streams where the fly life is somewhat scarce and the hatches small. Because of this comparative scarcity, the fish will gather in as much food as possible, knowing that there will not be a great deal of it. But in streams where there is an abundance of insect life and the hatches are large, it is a different story. The trout are much more selective and look their food over pretty carefully before taking it.

Most fishermen do not know which of these two conditions they are going to run into, and in fishing it is wise to be prepared for any eventuality.

The fact that you happen to be on a stream where trout are not selective is certainly not a good argument against knowing the natural flies, as well as their imitations. If a trout happens to be rising to anything that looks like food, it will certainly take a good imitation of the natural fly just as quickly as any other fly.

It should be remembered that the way small trout rise to artificials is no criterion, and dry flies should not be judged by their ability to catch the little fellows that do not know what it is all about.

A fly may take seven- to nine-inch trout, but

be well-nigh worthless as far as fooling those that are over a foot in length. I believe it is safe to say that from the standpoint of fun and satisfaction, trout from twelve inches up are the size that most of us want to catch.

Fishing pressure on most streams today is so great that a trout must have learned a great deal if it is to grow to fourteen inches. If he is dumb he does not grow to any size, and therefore larger trout are much more selective.

Smaller trout have not reached this degree of selectivity, especially in the streams where legal-sized fish are stocked. Most fish caught today are from seven to ten inches long and have not been away from the hatchery long enough to know what is going on. They will generally rise to anything that comes over them if it looks like food, and I have yet to find a real trout fisherman who got any satisfaction from catching them.

Please do not get the idea that by learning the May flies it will be possible to cope with every condition you will meet in fishing, or that you will be able to catch large trout every time you are on a stream when fish are feeding on duns that are emerging. If you do, you will be disappointed.

Even after a knowledge of May flies is attained, things will often work out other than expected.

I vividly recall an experience I had some years ago on one of my favorite pools. Above the pool is a nice riffle that is just right for *Ephemerella subvaria* (Hendrickson or Red Quill). It was just a bit early in the afternoon for these flies to emerge, so my companion and I started fishing with an imitation of the Hendrickson nymph.

We fished them for about a half hour before any naturals started coming, and when the hatch really got under way, trout were taking the duns regularly at the head of the pool.

We changed from nymph to Hendrickson dry flies, and for about an hour we had some excellent fishing. We did not keep track of the number we had caught, and we released all but five, but I should guess that between us we had caught between thirty-five and forty legal fish.

Each of us had hooked and lost a large trout, the size that does not always feed on the surface, but inasmuch as the Hendrickson hatch had just started, we knew that we could depend on them to come regularly for a few days. Of course, we planned to try for the two big fish again on the following day.

We were in the pool at about the same time the next day, but did no fishing, as we were interested in two specific fish and did not want to disturb the pool. There was a slight drizzle, and we felt that this was a good break for us because conditions would be even better than the previous day. Because the flies' wings would take longer to dry, we expected them to remain on the water longer, a condition that always produces better fly fishing.

When the hatch came the stream was covered with flies and fish were feeding all over the pool. It seemed that there were even more fish feeding than on the day before. It was not long before two that we assumed to be those we had hooked on the previous day started to work. They were in the same position and fed like large fish, so we felt quite confident that they were our friends.

After checking a couple of naturals we found that they were the females that were hatching, and put on Hendricksons. Because the natural was identical with those that we had found the day before, there was little doubt in our minds about raising the two large fish. There were so many flies on the stream that it was impossible to distinctly see fish take them, but from the way they were feeding, we were certain they were.

We both cast over our fish, and although they kept right on working, we could not raise either of them. I was sure that the identification had been correct, but try as we might, there was no luck. Because we had not put either of them down, we felt sure that it was not a case of faulty presentation, and our two friends kept working at regular intervals.

After about five minutes I decided that something was definitely wrong, and I moved farther up in the pool, where there were numerous smaller fish working. I cast over four different fish but had no better success, and was starting to think that I had made some mistake in technique, but could not dope out what it was.

In the meantime, my companion, as puzzled as I, had changed over to a Red Quill, the artificial of the male Hendrickson; but he still could not raise his fish.

Finally in desperation I took off the dry fly and put on a Hendrickson nymph—why, I do not know. I cast across the stream and let the nymph float down naturally. Just as it made the swing and started to come to the surface, a fish hit it as though his life depended on catching it. The manner of taking was identical to the way a fish rises for a dry fly, as there was a distinct "break," but not made by the trout's tail.

I called to my companion and told him what had happened, and continued to work downstream in the direction of my big fish. In five casts I caught three more fish, and was perfectly satisfied that we had found the answer. While I was releasing the last fish I heard a shout from farther down the pool and saw my partner having the time of his life with a heavy fish. Naturally, I went down to watch the fun, and after quite a few minutes he put his net under his beauty. It was a nineteen-inch brown that had apparently been living off the "fat of the land."

The commotion put my fish down, but we

were both satisfied, and tomorrow would be another day.

Why all the fish in that pool were passing up the duns they had taken so readily the previous day and were feeding instead on nymphs is a mystery to me. I had never seen this happen before, nor have I since, with this particular species of May fly. It is one of those mysteries of trout fishing, and I doubt that anyone can furnish a logical reason for it.

Incidentally, when the big fish was dressed we found that although his stomach was actually crammed with food, he had only three winged flies in it, the rest being nymphs of the Hendrickson fly. The flies that he had picked up were probably some that had drowned, and were floating just under the surface of the stream.

Another of the things that I am unable to find the answer to is the way trout sometimes act with *Iron fraudator* (Quill Gordon). It is the first important May fly to appear on almost all streams, and coming as it does early in the season, it has special appeal to the dry-fly fisherman. At this time of the year fish are starting to look for great quantities of food, and with higher water temperatures their appetites are large.

The normal emergence time of this fly is about one-thirty P.M., Eastern Standard Time, the hatch usually starting at about that time. Occasionally there will be a small hatch in the morning, between ten and eleven, depending on how cold the water is, but seldom have I seen fish feed on them.

Very often I have been on a pool in the morning when there was a fair-sized hatch, and yet there was not a fish feeding as nearly as I could determine. Still, in the very same pool in the afternoon the trout would take every fly that came over them, and they were identical with the flies that had been on the water in the morning. Strangely enough, they will not take a wet-fly imitation in the morning either, so that is not the answer.

All of us have sat in on discussions and friendly arguments pertaining to the way fish, trout in particular, look at things. When this answer is found, we will probably know why they are so selective on certain occasions and comparatively careless on others. This subject is probably one of the most controversial in trout fishing.

So far, I have not seen sufficient proof to satisfy me that anyone has even come close to the solution. There are many theories on the subject, but that is all they are, and I have yet to see one that could not be blown full of holes.

For example, many of us have placed flies in a small aquarium and looked up at them through the glass and water, in varying degrees of light, checking angles and so forth.

What does this amount to, after all? The way a fly floating thus appears to the human eye is one thing, but how can it be said positively that such is the way the same object will appear to a trout?

A large group of fishermen contend that trout cannot differentiate between one color and another. Because I cannot definitely prove they are wrong, I will not argue with them about it. However, if such is the case, I find it hard to explain why a trout will take one fly after having refused another that was dressed in exactly the same manner, with the exception of the body. For example, the size of the Hendrickson and Red Quill are the same, as are the hackles and wings. Why will fish refuse one and take the other? I do not know, do you? I doubt that there is a fisherman in the country who has not at some time or other had the same experience in selectivity.

Because I am on some trout stream nearly every day of the open season, I have a lot more time to experiment than do most people. I fool away so much time in this manner that I am only half as good a fisherman as I should be, for the amount of time I am at it. Nevertheless, I do not consider time spent in this way as wasted. We all fish because we get enjoyment out of it, and I get as much fun out of trying to solve some hitherto unexplained problem as I do in catching fish.

Although I have been studying it for quite a few years, I actually know nothing more about how a trout's vision compares to ours than I did when I started.

There is not a standard pattern of dry fly that I have not tried to improve upon, trying slightly different dressings. Except for minor changes, I have not been very successful. For example, in the tying of the Quill Gordon, I have found the fly more effective when tied with the quill from the eye of a peacock feather than when made with any other material. This in spite of the fact that the other dressing of the fly was exactly the same.

Whether or not this difference in effectiveness was due to the darker stripe in the peacock quill, giving the body of the fly the light and dark stripe, I do not profess to know. However, I am perfectly satisfied that the fly with this body, over a period of time, will produce larger and better fish.

If a trout's vision is even slightly comparable to ours, why is it that this same fly, the Quill Gordon, does not closely resemble to us the natural that it imitates? Fish will take it consistently when the natural is on the water, but I doubt if any person who did not know anything about the subject would ever think one a copy of the other, seeing them together.

This is true of most dry flies and nymphs, and to us they do not look anything like the naturals they represent, but they are apparently so suggestive to the fish that they are effective.

Having nothing definite to go by on this subject of vision and selectivity, I will continue to flounder along according to the experiences of others, and my own, until such time as a talking trout will be discovered that can give me the right dope. Possibly someday a mere mortal may discover the answer, but I hope that day never comes. Think of all the swell arguments we would miss!

Another matter that comes under this same heading is the proper color of leaders, from the standpoint of their visibility to trout.

One fisherman will swear that the most effective color is mist, and the next will argue that dark brown is the only shade to use. The result is that leaders are stained and dyed every color of the rainbow.

The fisherman who likes the darker shades says, "Look at that leader on the water, you cannot see it." Very true, we cannot, but we see it against the dark stream bottom. A fish, on the other hand, will see it from the opposite angle, looking up at it, with the sky as a background. According to that, it should be more readily seen by a trout than would one of mist color, or even natural gut.

As far as I am concerned, the color of a leader means very little. None of us, in fishing for a rising trout, would deliberately put the leader over the fish, knowing that it would become frightened. If, on the other hand, we are trying to "pound up" fish, we are putting our fly in the spots where we expect to find a trout.

It has been my experience that the only really

important thing about leaders is to remove the glare, and if gut is treated to remove this objectionable feature, color is of no consequence to me. Now that nylon has replaced gut, I find that Tintex dye does a nice job on the new material. I like green, but this is a matter of personal preference. The main thing is, it seems to cut down on glare. If you make your own tippets, they can be made more limp by boiling them during the dyeing process for exactly *one minute,* no longer. This will remove the wiriness from your 3X, 4X, and 5X tippets. But care must be used not to overboil them. One minute will not harm platyl in the least.

When you are next complaining about the selectivity of trout, bear this thought in mind: Were it not for this fortunate trait, how long would our stream fishing last? It would not be many years before our waters would be completely fished out, and I doubt that any of you would welcome that condition. In most cases, fish are scarce enough now in streams open to public fishing.

2

LIFE CYCLE OF THE MAY FLY

ALTHOUGH VERY FEW fishermen are interested in entomology, I believe that some knowledge of the life cycle of May flies will be of interest, as well as being an aid to fishing.

Because there are so many patterns of artificial flies sold, most fly fishermen are of the opinion that there are hundreds of species of important flies and that the study of them would take many years. They do not realize that by far the biggest percentage of flies sold are imitations of European flies, *none* of which are found in this country.

Obviously, it will be to our advantage to concentrate on those species that are native to our own streams, rather than those that do not occur here.

There are some May flies that emerge after dark, but they are of no value to most fly fishermen. This book will therefore only touch on those that we can expect to find during the daylight hours, and on which trout feed.

Fishermen will be pleasantly surprised to learn that there are less than a dozen species that are of importance to them. This does not mean that trout do not feed on the others, but for various reasons we can forget about them. For example, where a fly appears on a stream for only a day or two, the species is of little value to us. Figure out the chance in an entire season of your being there at the time they emerge. There are also some species that occur in such small numbers as to be of little or no importance, and certainly not worth imitating with an artificial fly.

Also, there are slight variations found that will not be mentioned, because except to the scientist they are of little value.

As the avowed purpose of this book is to eliminate as much as possible the number of patterns of artificial flies, only those naturals that appear in good quantities every season will be described.

It is surprising how few fishermen realize that most of a May fly's life is spent underwater, and I have even had occasions where it was hard to convince a fisherman that such was the case. Strangely enough, if the nymph of the May fly is left out of water it will die, but when the fly itself emerges, it will die if it is submerged in water.

The eggs of May flies are deposited in the streams in different ways. In some species, the female drops down to the surface of the stream, touching the water, whereby the eggs are washed off. Others carry them in small orange- or lemon-colored masses, which most of us are familiar with, and drop them into the stream while flying over it.

Unfortunately, many of these eggs never get into the stream, because for some unknown reason many of the females mistake the highways, especially those constructed of macadam, for the stream. This is particularly true if the roads are wet, and in flying about, the flies are smashed against our windshields, headlights, and grilles. Anyone driving near streams in the late spring and summer has had this experience, and we know what a job it is to remove the eggs when they have dried. You can well imagine that because of this, fly life in our streams has been reduced to a considerable degree.

After being deposited in the water, the egg masses disintegrate and sink to the bottom of the stream, where in due time they hatch. The tiny nymphs then crawl under stones in the riffles, burrow in the silt, or cling to the underside of submerged logs or vegetation along the stream banks. They feed on minute vegetation and go through a succession of molts, throwing off their outer covering as they outgrow it.

When the nymphs have attained their full growth, they do one of several things, depending on the species. Some swim or crawl to shore, where the waters are more still, remaining under stones until their emergence periods arrive. Others crawl from under the stone, going to the downstream side of it, and remain there until the nymph case opens and the fly emerges.

The nymphs of some species are very active for some minutes prior to their emergence, and when the time arrives for the nymph to leave its nymphal shuck, it will float on the surface for quite some distance, struggling all the while to force open the nymph case, which splits open at the back.

When the insect emerges from its nymph case, it is known to fishermen as a *dun,* owing more or less to the dull appearance of the fly's wings. At this stage it is a rather slow flyer and is easy to catch. It leaves the stream, and if lucky, it will reach a tree or bush, where it will remain for a period up to twenty-four hours. During this time a complete transformation takes place, and during this stage of its metamorphosis develops breeding organs. The fly is then known as a *spinner,* so called on account of its actions in flight.

In almost all cases there is a great difference in the appearance of the dun and the corresponding spinner. The wings of the latter are clear, whereas those of the dun were dull. The bodies of the spinners are more slender, and the tails greatly enlarged. Where the dun was slow in flight, the spinner is very fast, having a peculiar up-and-down flight, and is very difficult to catch.

The spinners then complete the cycle by procreation. Mating actually takes place in the air, the male approaching the female from below. It hangs to the female by means of forceps at the end of its body and by grasping the female by its feet, flight being uninterrupted.

After the eggs are fertilized, the female returns to the stream (unless she makes a mistake and goes to the highway instead), where the eggs are deposited.

The flies live only a very short time, and they cannot eat, because their mouths are wasted away in their metamorphosis.

In most cases spinners are of little value to fly fishermen. The transformation from the dun is such that there is very little left in the way of food for fish, and because of their erratic manner of flight, fish do not have much of an opportunity to get them until they are spent.

The only nutritive value to fish is in the female before she has deposited her eggs, and very few of them fall into the stream until they are completely spent. Because these spent flies do not usually get into the stream until nearly dark, there is very little point in trying to copy them, and as a rule fish will not bother with spinners if they can get duns.

As with all rules, there are exceptions to this one. In the case of the fly known as the Green Drake, the spinner is known as the Coffin Fly, and is probably a familiar insect to most fishermen. Trout seem to relish the female spinner, provided she still has eggs in her and is not spent.

These flies dip their eggs on the water, and it is probably at such times that the trout catch them. On the other hand, they will pay absolutely no attention to the male. How fish can differentiate between the two I do not know, although there is a slight difference in color. The body of the female, because of the eggs, has a slight yellow cast, whereas that of the male is white.

Some may ridicule this statement, feeling that I am giving trout credit for possessing greater intelligence, or what have you, than they do. However, I have witnessed this occurrence so often that I know it is true in most cases. Further proof can be had by studying the stomach contents of a trout that has been feeding on these spinners. Unless I am greatly mistaken, you will note that the spinners found there will contain eggs.

Another spinner that trout seem to relish is that of *Isonychia bicolor*. It too is a large fly, and fish take it quite readily. A partial explanation of this no doubt lies in the fact that unlike most May flies, both the dun and spinner of *Isonychia* are very apt to be found on the stream at the same time.

With most May flies, the dun and spinner are decidedly different in appearance, but not so with this species. Except for their wings, they are very similar. The spinner, of course, has the usual clear wing, whereas the dun's is very dull.

Spinners probably bother fishermen more than anything else that they encounter in their fishing experiences, and yet the answer is very simple.

All of us have been on a stream at some time, generally in the evening, when the air was full of flies, but there were no fish rising. This puzzles fishermen to such an extent that they will often remark that there are no fish in the stream, because if there were they would be feeding with all those flies. The reason is, of course, that the flies are spinners, and are in the air, *not* on the water, so the fish cannot get them even if they want to.

With duns, on the other hand, fish get an opportunity to catch them, for duns cannot leave the water until their wings are thoroughly dry. If you watch a dun when it does leave the water, you will notice that it never tarries in one spot. It will make a beeline for some tree or bush.

There are some streams where in the latter

months of the season the water heats to such a degree that trout do little or no feeding on the surface during the day. At such times, their activity is confined to late evening and night, when the water cools.

If the water temperature is such that no duns emerge during the late evening at the time the fish are leaving the deeper waters of pools to search for food, trout will often pick up spinners that they normally would not touch. These are the spinners of the duns that emerged the previous day.

Because fish are hungry and just starting to feed, they will pick up these spent flies. It has been my experience that at such times trout are extremely selective, and I know of no condition where they are harder to take. When they are feeding on these spinners in flat water, they seem to do a lot of "cruising," and they have no fixed feeding position. First they will dimple in one spot, and then swim along and suck in a spinner eight or ten feet away.

At such times every cast must be well-nigh perfect, and an extra-long leader will be a distinct advantage. The fisherman must stand perfectly still, so as not to make the slightest ripple on the surface, and after casting, the fly must be left to float just as long as it will, on the chance that the "cruiser" may see and rise to it.

In studying the actions of fish at such times, I have seen them rise very leisurely to a fly, look it over for a matter of seconds before either taking or splashing it. Usually if they see that it is not the real McCoy, they will head for the deep waters as though possessed of the devil. They apparently know from past experience that a spent fly will not leave the water, and they can take as much time as they want to check on it.

Because this kind of fishing is the most uncertain of all, I will not go into detail on dressings for spinners. For every species of May fly that exists, there is of course a spinner, and it is my sincere belief that they are not worth bothering with on the whole.

With normal water temperatures there are generally hatches of duns in the evening, and when they do appear, fish will not spend any time on spinners, taking instead the more *meaty* flies.

One fly that I have found quite effective when fish are feeding on spinners is tied very similarly to the Red Quill, described later, except that it should be tied very sparse and with no wings, preferably on a No. 14 hook. The dun hackles should be the lightest shade obtainable.

May flies emerge in regular order every season, on all streams, and this is probably the only thing in trout fishing that we can definitely depend on. You can bet your last dollar that Hendricksons will follow Quill Gordons, and so on right down the line, and there is never the slightest deviation in the rotation on any stream.

It is impossible to tell the date that flies will make their first appearance on a stream, as this is determined by water temperature. For example, flies will emerge at an earlier date in Pennsylvania than in New York, because the streams warm up sooner. Similarly, in mountainous areas they will come later than in streams in the lowlands.

Flies seldom appear on the streams until the water temperature has reached fifty degrees, and they do not often emerge when it gets above seventy.

The emergence tables that appear later pertain to *normal* stream conditions. On cloudy days, or when streams are high and off color, often flies that normally emerge in the evening will be present at almost any time of the day. This is especially true of dark days when you will often find such species as *Ephemerella dorothea, Isonychia bicolor, Potamanthus distinctus, Ephemera varia* —all normal evening emergers.

3

COLLECTING

DURING THE FIRST few years that I studied insect life on the various streams, I found that the May flies apparently appeared in regular order every year, in each stream checked.

In order to determine positively that such was the case, I spent three entire fishing seasons doing little other than collecting specimens on a typical trout stream located in New York State. It is the Schoharie Creek, and is ideal for the purpose.

It has every conceivable type of water, from fast rocky stretches to long flat pools. This was a very important factor, because certain May flies habitate one portion of the stream, while others require a condition just the opposite.

From a fishing standpoint, the three years spent on this work were wasted. It was necessary to spend every day doing the collecting, so that I could be certain the record was complete. I was anxious to get as many flies as possible, to make sure that no species was missed. It was also important to have a positive record of the emergence dates.

Other fishermen encountered on the stream naturally thought I was crazy, chasing "those bugs" when there was a good feed of fish. Quite often apologies were in order, for I fear that my stream manners were on occasion not what they should have been, but when I was chasing a fly all else was forgotten.

Why I carried my rod and other fishing equipment I do not know, unless I felt that a fisherman could get away with things that might otherwise be considered the act of a "nut."

Very often I was tempted to give the whole thing up, feeling that the results would not be worth the effort. I remember one day in particular. I saw a dun leave the water, and it was getting elevation fast. I ran toward it and jumped up, trying to catch it in my hat. To this day I do not know whether or not I caught it, for when my feet came down, one landed on a very slippery stone, and the next thing I knew I was in the "drink." The soaking would not have bothered me, but a broken rod is far from a cause for joy.

To the best of my knowledge, no such collection was ever made before, covering every day of the season between April and July. Believing it to be of general interest, I am listing below the results of my three-year study of those flies that are of importance to fishermen.

Iron fraudator (Quill Gordon) 	(1) April	28, 29, 30
	May	2, 4, 5, 6, 7, 9, 16
	(2) May	6, 7, 9, 10, 13, 18, 21, 24, 25
	(3) April	22, 23, 28, 29
	May	1, 2, 3, 6, 8, 9, 10, 11, 12, 13, 14, 21, 22, 28
Ephemerella subvaria (Hendrickson— Red Quill) 	(1) May	2, 4, 5, 6, 7, 8, 16
	(2) May	12, 13, 17, 21, 28, 29
	(3) April	29
	May	1, 2, 3, 6, 8, 10, 20, 22

Ephemerella dorothea
(Small Cream Variant)

(1) May 16, 17, 18,
         21, 22, 25
(2) June 8, 13
(3) May 28
    June 7, 30
    July 4

Iron humerelis
(Small Cream Variant)

(1) May 17, 23
    June 6, 7, 22, 27,
          28
    July 8
(2) May 31
    June 11, 26
    July 9, 10, 13, 15
(3) May 5, 8, 9, 12,
         19, 21
    June 3, 5, 7, 9, 11,
          19, 22, 26
    July 4, 10
    Aug. 20, 26, 27

Blasturus cupidas
(Red Quill)

(1) May 29
(2) May 6, 9, 10, 21,
         22, 26, 29, 31
    June 2, 4, 5, 8
(3) May 2, 6, 10, 11,
         12, 13, 14
    June 3, 7

Stenonema vicarium   (1) May   12, 13, 14,
(American March Brown)   16, 17, 18,
                                     21, 22, 23,
                                     24, 25, 27

                          (2) May   25, 30
                              June 6, 12, 13
                          (3) May   3, 6, 8, 9, 11,
                                     12, 13, 14,
                                     21, 29, 30, 31
                              June 2, 3, 5

Stenonema fuscum   (1) May   11, 22, 25,
(Grey Fox)   27, 28, 29,
                                     30, 31
                              June 1, 4, 5, 7

                          (2) June 4, 6, 8, 13, 23
                              July 18
                          (3) May   13, 14, 20, 28
                              June 3, 7, 18, 21

Stenonema canadensis   (1) May   22, 23, 24,
(Light Cahill)   25, 29, 30,
                                     31
                              June 3, 4, 5, 6, 8,
                                     9, 11, 22, 25,
                                     26, 29

                              July 1, 5, 7, 9, 13
                                     15
                          (2) June 5, 6, 11, 13,
                                     16, 23, 24
                              July 2, 6, 9, 10,
                                     13, 15, 25
                          (3) June 22, 30

Stenonema interpunc-
  tatum
(no value to fishermen)

(1) May 20
    June 7
(2) June 3, 4, 5, 11, 13
(3) July 4, 16

Isonychia bicolor
(Dun Variant)

(1) May 22, 24, 25,
         29, 31
    June 3, 5, 6, 8, 11,
          13, 17, 22,
          26, 27, 28, 30
    July 30
(2) May 13, 18, 19
    June 4, 9, 12
(3) May 28, 29, 30, 31
    June 2, 3, 4, 5, 7,
          11, 18, 26, 30
    July 3, 6, 7
    Aug. 14, 20, 21, 26

Ephemera guttulata
(Large Grey Fox
  Variant)

(1) May 18, 22, 24,
         25, 26, 29
    June 1
(2) June 2, 4, 9
(3) May 30, 31
    June 2, 4

Potamanthus distinctus
(Cream Variant)

(1)	June	13, 17, 28
	July	13, 15
(2)	July	6, 13, 17
(3)	June	19, 21, 22, 23, 26
	July	3, 6, 7, 10, 16

All of the flies listed are of importance to the fly fisherman with the exception of *Stenonema interpunctatum*. It is mentioned only because it is a fly that is often brought to me for identification, its colors being rather pretty. The wings are lemon yellow and the body coral, deeper in the female than the male. It is an evening emerger, and does not seem to occur in as many streams as the rest of the *Stenonema* group. I have never found it actually hatching, so it is probably quite late at night before it appears.

It will be noted that there are gaps in the collection dates of the various flies. For example, the first year's record of *P. distinctus* shows that I found flies on June 13, 17, and 28. Probably flies emerged every day between those dates, and I just did not happen to be on a portion of the stream where they were hatching.

Most likely, many readers will want to do a bit of collecting of their own, either for identification purposes or to start a small collection to show their friends.

The most practical receptacles are small bottles with wide mouths. The liquid used should completely fill the bottles, as May flies are very delicate. There will be less breakage when they are carried in a full bottle.

The following solution is recommended for flies:

1 part formaldehyde (40 percent solution), 19 parts distilled water.

The following is for nymphs:

1 part formaldehyde (40 percent solution), 10 parts distilled water.

Because nymphs feed entirely on vegetable matter, the colors of May flies fade very soon, but in most cases characteristic markings will remain visible. A magnifying glass of low power will be of assistance in the task of identification.

4

MAY-FLY MIDGETS

THERE IS ONE group of May flies that will not be taken up in detail, but which I feel should be mentioned briefly.

They are the tiny duns that are represented by dry flies tied on size 18 or 20 hooks. These little insects have plagued every fisherman at some time or other, and hardly need any description. They are not to be confused with midges, very tiny insects that are *not* May flies.

Their size is their distinguishing characteristic, and as a rule when they are on the water and fish are feeding on them, you will not take many fish if you use a fly larger than a size 18.

What there is about these little creatures that makes them appeal to trout, I do not profess to know. On many occasions I have seen really large trout rising for them, when it seemed that they must burn up more energy in rising for the fly than it was worth. The strangest thing of all is why when they are feeding on these small duns they will pass up a larger natural, and right behind it take another small one.

I ran into a week of this fishing some seasons ago, and was surely glad when it ended. Every day these little devils would start to hatch at about noon, and they were on the water by the thousand. Much to everyone's disgust, the fish fed on them in the pockets and tails of runs, but *not* in the pools. It is tough enough to fish a No. 18 fly in flat water, with perfect light conditions, and of course it is still worse in the pockets. Fishing such a small fly in fast water is something.

Most fishermen that I have met do the same thing when running into this condition. Instead of putting on the fly that they know will take fish, they put on a 16 or 14, which they know from past experience will not work. They say hope springs eternal in the breast of man, and I guess it is particularly true in the case of trout fishermen.

It is seldom that a large fly will prove effective when trout are taking these midgets. Fish will as a rule either disregard the larger dry fly or else come up and "nudge" it. I think that most anglers will agree that this is just about the most exasperating fishing, and there is little fun in fishing a fly that cannot be seen, nine casts out of ten. If we are fortunate enough to be able to follow our fly, most of us make the same mistake and strike both too hard and too fast, forgetting that our hook is very small.

If you want to get palpitation of the heart, hook a three-pound trout on one of these small flies. Every move the fish makes, you expect him to get off, and it really takes some careful handling to bring him to net. Catching a two-pound trout on one of these flies gives me a great deal more satisfaction than a four-pounder on a No. 12.

Quite often there are evening hatches of these little May flies, but at such times the fish usually feed in the pools. This is much easier fishing, because even though we cannot always see our fly, we know approximately where it is, by the wake made by the leader on the water when it reaches the surface. This is usually more productive than pocket and run fishing with the small flies, with a better percentage of fish hooked and landed.

It has been my experience that when fish are feeding on these little insects, they are not the least bit selective as to color, and will take almost any fly, provided it is small enough.

For the fisherman who has not encountered this kind of fishing, I will give one bit of advice.

When you are fishing with these small flies and the trout take them, do not raise your rod tip to set the hook as fast as you would if fishing a fly with a 12 or 14 hook. This will require considerable self-control, but it will pay mighty good dividends. I have found that the more time between the strike and the set of the hook—within reason, of course—the deeper the fish will be hooked. Very often I have caught large fish on these small flies, and found they were hooked well back in the throat, which of course is a big help.

The main hatch of these small duns follows the *Stenonemas,* starting at about noon, and they emerge for over an hour. The hatch usually continues for about one week.

If you tie your own flies, try a Dun Variant tied on a No. 18 hook, leaving off wings. This is much more easily tied than a regular winged fly, and a bit easier to see. No body is necessary on this fly, so it is really a cinch to make. The hackle size should be about the same as would normally be used on a No. 14 Quill Gordon, preferably a natural dun.

5

QUILL GORDON

(Iron Fraudator)

Iron fraudator ♀ Subimago.

HOW I WELCOME the day this fly makes its first appearance each season, for it means that at long last dry-fly fishing has started.

It is the first May fly of consequence to emerge, coming rather early in the season, often appearing when the air is so cold that few of the flies are able to leave the water, being numb and unable to fly.

When this condition exists in the streams where they are plentiful, I have seen so many of them floating downstream that in spite of the care I used in casting I could not locate my own fly.

At such times trout will usually gorge themselves, taking advantage of the fly's inability to leave the water. Catching fish under such conditions is more difficult than it sounds, because of the difficulty of finding the artificial among the dozens of naturals. It is very hard to tell whether a fish has taken a natural or your artificial, and fishermen must be right on their toes every minute.

I will never forget such a day as that, fishing with a friend who had only had a very small amount of dry-fly experience, and had never seen a real "feed." When instructing him the season before, I had told him about some of the occasions when the stream seems to boil with fish, but I think that there was a very large doubt in his mind about it.

We had hardly arrived at the portion of the stream that we intended to fish before I noticed the swallows dipping down to the water. As any fisherman would be, I was suspicious that a hatch had started, for swallows do not dive to the stream to clean their teeth. Promptly getting our rods strung up and leaders on, we put on Quill Gordons, crossed the stream, and moved up about thirty yards to a good pool that had a grand riffle coming into it.

It did not take long to see what the swallows were so interested in, and within ten minutes the stream was simply covered with naturals, and fish boiling all over the place.

There was a nasty downstream wind blowing, and it was simply impossible to put a fly where you wanted. Because it was so cold that flies were unable to leave the water, catching a fish was purely a matter of luck, owing to the difficulty in locating the artificial. The Quill Gordon is a hard fly to see under perfect conditions, but on a dark day, with a stiff wind blowing, it is next to impossible to find.

Never having seen such a sight, my friend was so excited he hardly knew what he was doing. A fish would come up in front of him, and he would try to put the fly there. Then one would come up to his right, and over to the right would go the fly, and if one came up to his left, another cast would be made. There was just no point in trying to tell him anything, for he was so excited that he paid no attention to me. Then when a fish took his fly, he did not realize it until he felt the line tighten, and as you can well imagine, he hit him just as hard as he could, leaving his fly in the fish. He put on a new fly, and I will admit that the air was so darn cold that his job was a mean one. After getting it on, he apparently was watching the stream when he started to cut the excess gut from his fly, for when he cast, he found much to his sorrow that he had cut the leader very close to the line. He started in to shore, in one devil of a hurry to put on a new leader, still looking at the working fish instead of where he was going, and the next thing I knew there was a splash, and one very wet fisherman was picking himself up when I turned around, wader legs bulging with water.

I was a bit worried for fear he would catch cold and suggested that we go home so that he could change his clothes, but he said that as far as he was concerned he would rather have pneumonia than miss what he was seeing in the stream.

Many of you may be grinning at this chap's experience; you may have had almost the same thing occur to you. I have seen seasoned fishermen who have been at the game for many years get darned near as excited to this day when the fish start to work in that manner, and I feel sorry for the man who does not get a bit of a tingle when he hits it that way.

This natural does not require high water temperatures as do most species. I generally look for them when the water has warmed to the point where the stream thermometer reaches the fifty mark and stays there for a couple of days.

Strangely enough, after the hatch has started the weather does not affect them if it turns colder. Often I have seen the water temperature drop to as low as thirty-six at night, but it did not keep the flies from emerging the next day, with the water still below forty-five in the afternoon.

It took me quite a few years to learn this important fact. Like most fishermen, I supposed that the weather had to be decent before flies would hatch, and if there happened to be a cold raw wind blowing, and the day was generally unpleasant, I would assume that it was not the kind of day to expect to find flies on the water.

It will be well worth your while to remember that after Quill Gordons have started to appear, it will pay to be on the stream, in spite of the weather. Bear in mind that cold or wet weather is a distinct advantage to you when this fly is on the water, and you will experience some of the finest days you have ever seen with a dry fly.

It is regrettable that on such days so few of the naturals leave the stream, owing to cold or wet conditions. I have seen thousands of them float downstream, being too cold to fly, and finish up being carried to a very turbulent piece of water below, where those that were not picked up by fish were drowned.

Because this is the first May fly of any size to appear in the spring, it is of great importance to the dry-fly fisherman. It comes at a time when fish are still hungry, having eaten very little during the winter months, and of course their appetites increase as the water warms. This results in a field day for the trout when the flies start to emerge. And, too, fish are a bit more careless early in the season, having forgotten some of their past lessons.

Another factor that is an advantage to the fisherman is the amount of water in the streams under normal conditions in early spring. With comparatively high water, trout are less shy than they are later in the season, when the streams are lower.

The first Quill Gordon was tied by Theodore Gordon, and very few changes have been made in his original dressing. Whether or not *Iron fraudator* was the natural Mr. Gordon copied, I do not know, but the fly bearing his name will take fish consistently when this May fly is on the water.

Trout tend to be very selective when feeding on this fly, and I would advise fishermen who get on the streams early in the season to have a supply of them when starting out. On many occasions I have seen fish refuse any other artificial.

The female is larger and slightly lighter in color than the male, but my experience has been that trout will take a properly tied Quill Gordon with either light or dark dun hackles.

Iron fraudator has two tails and has brown heart-shaped markings on the legs, visible to the naked eye.

With normal water conditions, they emerge at about one-thirty P.M., the main hatch coming at that time. As mentioned previously, there may be a small hatch in the morning, but the one in the afternoon is of most importance to fishermen.

Higher than normal water temperatures have an adverse effect on this fly, as with all May flies. I recall one season when the streams were much lower than normal in the spring, as there had been very little snow in the mountains and the spring rains failed to materialize. Because the weather had been unusually mild and dry, the streams were as low as they would generally be in mid-June.

Quill Gordons started to emerge on April 22, nearly two weeks before the average date, and came at about their regular hour for two days.

On the third day it was extremely warm, and the water temperature was quite a bit higher than normal for the time of the year. A companion and I were on the stream at about twelve-forty-five, each on a different part of the stream, and we had agreed to get together again at five P.M.

There being no flies on the water when I reached the stream, and no sign of fish working, I put on a wet Quill Gordon. I took a few small fish, but as the anticipated hour arrived and no flies showed up, it had me puzzled. I knew that the part of the stream that I was fishing was good water for *Iron fraudator,* and there were also some good trout there, but try as I might with wet, dry, and bucktail, all that I could interest were small fish up to nine inches.

The weather was ideal, one of those spring days when we expect all of nature to be on the move; certainly the kind of day to expect good fly fishing. And as the water was only sixty, I did not understand why the flies did not come.

I was not sorry when the hour came for our meeting. My friend had no better luck than I, and if anything he was a bit more disgusted. We had about all the fishing we wanted for a while, and returned home for a bite to eat, and no doubt for one or two of those things that we drink to pick up our spirits.

After stowing away some groceries I suggested that we go back to the stream, but my partner had sufficient for one day. Although I could not coax him to get into his waders again, he did agree to drive to one of our pet pools to see what, if anything, was doing. I had a hunch that the unseasonable heat had put the flies back and they would come in the evening, although I had never seen this happen with Quill Gordons, other than a few stragglers.

We sat on a ledge, legs dangling down toward the pool, and had been there only a few minutes when a few fish started dimpling right in front of us. I moved along the ledge to an eddy, and sure enough, my hunch had been right, for there were some Quill Gordons.

It was just plain dumb luck that we had all of our equipment in the car, with the exception of our waders and shoes, but as you can well imagine that slight detail did not worry us, and in just a few minutes we were in action.

We had some of the nicest fishing one could wish, and my friend wound up by tying into one the size of which you read about but seldom see. Although neither of us saw the fish at any time, I feel certain from the way it acted that it was the largest trout that I had ever seen rise to a dry fly. The fish wound up breaking the rod tip, and with that Mr. Trout just went places, and of course took a bit of leader and fly for a souvenir.

This was the first and one of the very few times that I have seen the main hatch of these flies emerging at night. More often than not, the streams are above normal rather than below normal at the time they hatch.

The dressing for Quill Gordon follows:

Wings—flank feather of mandarin or wood duck
Body—quill from peacock eye, light
Hackle—natural blue dun, medium
Tail—few wisps blue dun barb or spade hackle
Hook—No. 12 or 14

As the peacock quills are somewhat delicate, I suggest that the body be wound with extra-fine gold wire, and that care be taken to cover the dark portion of the quill rather than the light. Ribbing the quill in this manner will assure longer service from the fly.

There is another May fly, very similar to *Iron fraudator,* which is much more prevalent in the West than in the East. It is known as *Rhithrogena* and is rather common in Utah and California and other western states. The nymphs can be distinguished very readily by the red gills.

An imitation of the fly has been found very effective tied the same as a Quill Gordon on size 10 and 12 hooks.

6

HENDRICKSON AND RED QUILL

(Ephemerella Subvaria)

Ephemerella subvaria ♂ Subimago.

THE SECOND FLY of importance is *Ephemerella subvaria;* strangely enough, it is represented by two artificials. The Hendrickson represents the female, the Red Quill the male.

This is the only May fly that requires a distinction in the artificial between the male and female, but there is a marked difference in the naturals, not so much in their markings and color as their habits. As a rule, the male will emerge on one riffle, the female on another, and trout are usually selective to such an extent that they will only take a Hendrickson if they are feeding on the female, or a Red Quill if the opposite is the case.

When it is considered that the only difference in the dressing of the two flies is in the body, it is hard to understand this selectivity. Often I have been unable to raise fish to a Red Quill, changed to a Hendrickson, and had good luck. To prove the point, I have again changed to the Red Quill, have not been able to raise another fish, and have again gone back to a Hendrickson, and again caught fish. Those trout fishermen who contend that fish cannot distinguish color and are not selective on a hatch would have a hard time explaining away the above condition.

This may be easier to understand when it is realized that usually the male of this fly emerges in a different part of the stream than the female. For example, mostly females may be coming off one riffle, and the next riffle upstream would produce almost all males. To my knowledge, no other May fly has this peculiarity.

The wings of this natural are smoky-blue dun color, similar to those of Quill Gordon. There is considerable variation in the shade in the various specimens that I have collected. It has three tails that are specked, as compared with only two on *Iron fraudator*. The body of the male is of a distinctly more reddish shade than the female.

This fly immediately follows Quill Gordon, as a rule overlapping it. The hatch generally starts at about two P.M., a bit later than the former fly, but it has been my experience that when *Ephem-erella* starts, fish will have little to do with *Iron* during the hatch. Why they should be so selective, with so little difference in the artificials, I cannot attempt to explain. When it is realized that the only real difference in the tying of Quill Gordon, Red Quill, and Hendrickson is in the body, it is doubly puzzling. There are no hard and fast rules for this selectivity, and I do not mean to imply that it is always the case, but in my experience it has been the rule and not the exception.

The first artificial tied to imitate this May fly, and given the name Hendrickson, was tied by Mr. Roy Steenrod, of Liberty, New York. Although he originated his fly some years ago, the dressing has not been improved upon or changed to any great extent up to the present.

The Hendrickson dressing I like follows:

Wings—flank feather mandarin or wood-duck drake
Body—pink fur from vixen of red fox
    (color comes from urine burns)
Hackle—natural blue dun
Tail—few wisps dun spade or barb feather
Hook—No. 12

Mr. Steenrod's dressing called for wood-duck feathers for the wings, but as our lawmakers at one time frowned on the use of this plumage, mandarin may be substituted. His dressing for the body called for fawn belly fur, and although the difference is slight, I have had a bit better success with fur of a slightly pinkish cast.

There is another and older fly that apparently was originally tied to imitate *E. subvaria,* which we know as the Whirling Dun. I do not like it as well, because it definitely will not hold up as well, nor do I believe it will take fish as consistently. Many old-timers swear by the good old Whirling Dun, and for my part they are as much entitled to their opinion as I am to mine.

The name Red Quill is an old one, having been given to an English fly many years ago. I took the liberty of borrowing it a few years ago when I started tying a fly to represent the male *E. subvaria.* The fly is like Mr. Steenrod's, except for the body.

The dressing of the Red Quill follows:

Wings—flank feather of mandarin or wood-duck drake

Body—quill of large hackle feather from Rhode Island Red cock, stripped and well soaked

Hackle—natural blue dun

Tail—few wisps of dun spade or barb feather

Hook—No. 12

Because the body is made from a red quill,

this name was given the fly. To the best of my knowledge, I must plead guilty to being the first to use this material for bodies in flies. If someone else used it prior to 1933, and I am taking credit that rightfully belongs to another, I extend my humble apology. In checking I find no mention of it in any book, including Mr. Bergman's fine work *Trout*. This book contains over five hundred descriptions of wet and dry flies, but no mention is made of quills from hackles for body materials.

Care must be exercised in using these quills for fly-tying, for if they are wound dry they are apt to crack. This may not show up immediately, but they will break and unwind after the fly has been fished with for a short time. If they are soaked overnight, little if any trouble will be experienced with them. After the fly is made and the body thoroughly dry, it should be lacquered twice, after which it makes a very attractive and lifelike fly. For late-season fishing in low water I have found a sparsely tied Red Quill on a No. 14 or No. 16 hook a most effective fly.

Most fly-tyers use mandarin for the tails of Hendrickson, and while it is true that both it and the Red Quill would look more like the natural fly with this material, I prefer the recommended feathers. I am perfectly satisfied that there is no difference from the standpoint of taking trout, but there is no comparison in the way barbs or spades float and stand up.

When the spinners of this fly return to the stream it is quite a sight. They usually appear about an hour after the hatch has finished. Those that return to the stream on one day are the flies that had emerged on the previous day.

After they have mated, the females carrying their eggs return to the stream, and for some reason always attempt to fly upstream, even to the point of bucking a downstream wind. They come in swarms, bodies in a perpendicular position, with the small yellow balls of eggs carried at the end of the body. They do not dip off their eggs, but drop them into the water in the riffles.

Trout rarely show any interest in these spinners, probably because they return to the stream a short time after the emergence of the duns, upon which the fish have fed.

This fly like all others is affected by high water temperatures. On streams that tend to heat up, it will often emerge in the evening instead of its normal emergence time in the afternoon. Under normal conditions it will appear at almost exactly the same time every afternoon, to such an extent that I have heard many fishermen remark that you could almost set your watch by it.

There is another fly that emerges at about the same time, and in some sections it might be mistaken for *E. subvaria*. This fly is *Blasturus cupidas,* and is of comparatively small value. It can readily be distinguished from *E. subvaria* by a characteristic of its tail. Although both flies have three tails, the center one of *Blasturus* is shorter than the other two.

There are two smaller flies that are often found on the water at about the same time of year as *E. subvaria,* and both are of interest to the fisherman.

One is *Ephemerella dorothea,* the other *Iron humerelis.* Both are light-colored flies, and although there are several flies tied to imitate them, I have never found anything that suited me as well as a Cream Variant, tied with small hackles on a No. 16 hook.

I have found that this imitation will work well for both naturals, and the Variant is much more practical, because it can be seen better. As both of these naturals appear on the stream in the evening, when winged flies are rather difficult to see, the Variant can be fished later—when a winged fly could not be seen.

Another reason for my partiality to the Cream Variant is that it works well for several other very light-colored flies that appear at different times throughout the entire season. This follows in line with the purpose of the book—to do away with as many patterns as is practical.

7

AMERICAN MARCH BROWN

(Stenonema Vicarium)

Stenonema vicarium ♀ Subimago.

THIS IS THE first of the very important *Stenonema* group to make its appearance, and it is considered by many fishermen the most important fly that we have.

It is more commonly called the "May fly," but the writer does not care for this name, because all of the upright-winged flies are true May flies.

There are several flies in this group, but none so important to both the fish and fishermen as the March Brown. It is very abundant in almost all streams, and trout are equally as fond of the nymph as the winged fly.

Being a large and meaty morsel, it appeals to the large trout as well as to those of smaller size, and very often I have located large fish feeding on March Browns that were not active when either Hendricksons or Quill Gordons were on the water.

S. vicarium is one of the easiest of the May flies to identify, and once it is seen it should not be confused with any other fly. It is the first really large fly of the season, and unlike the preceding species, has mottled brown wings.

One positive means of identification is the position in which its wings are held when at rest, a characteristic of all flies in the *Stenonema* family. Instead of being straight upright, as most May flies, this one carries its wings slanted back, so much so that no other fly should be mistaken for it.

Another distinguishing characteristic is the brown markings on the insect's legs, which is true of the entire *Stenonema* group.

Several days before the flies are ready to emerge the nymphs move to the more still waters along shore, where they remain until Mother Nature gives them the "go" sign. They can be studied very easily at this time, and almost every flat stone along shore will harbor from one to eight of these insects. As the stone is picked up, some will scurry to the opposite side and others will play possum, but the movement of their gills shows them to be other than dead. Peculiarly enough, this nymph has three tails, whereas the fly when it emerges has only two.

Unlike *Iron* and *Ephemerella,* the March Brown does not have any regular emerging time. The flies generally start appearing about two hours before noon and continue hatching sporadically most of the day. Should the water temperature be too high, there would be only one fairly large hatch, coming as a rule late in the day. Their emerging can definitely be called sporadic.

How any of these flies live to procreate is a mystery. From the time the nymphs leave their hiding places under the stones to the time they reach the trees they are easy prey for fish and birds, and actually seem to dare their enemies to come and catch them.

After the nymph swims to the surface, it floats along, wiggling for all it is worth, trying to force open its case. Naturally, trout take large numbers of them at this time. They take much longer to emerge than do most flies, and often when one has reached the surface in a pool I have timed it and found that it took about ten minutes to escape from its shuck.

When the fly finally breaks out, it usually uses its nymph case as a raft, floating downstream on it, until it believes its wings to be dry. It is rarely that this fly is successful in its first attempt at flight, usually going only a few feet before dropping back onto the water. Often the fly will make six or seven such attempts, and this activity on the part of the fly makes it especially attractive to trout. If the fly is successful in leaving the stream, more often than not it will be a victim of a swallow or some other bird, as it is a very slow-flying creature.

It has been my experience that trout are apt to feed on these flies at any time, having no regular feeding period. Strangely enough, they may go for hours before taking one off the surface, despite the fact that fairly large numbers are emerging.

Very often they will ignore the mature insects in the morning but feed on nymphs, taking some and passing up others. Then in the afternoon they may start working on the surface, and rise to every natural that comes into their range of vision. Often they will spend only a few minutes on the nymphs and go right to work on the flies, another of the idiosyncrasies of trout fishing.

I once ran into a different experience when March Browns were on the water. Because of drought conditions of the previous year, fly life on the stream I was fishing was less plentiful than normal. Starting out with two friends in the morning, I fished hard and had very little luck, taking only a few small trout, none over nine inches. Although there were a few flies appearing on and off, fish showed no interest in them, and I had seen only one fish rise all morning.

We met at noon and had our lunch, after which each of us picked a portion of the stream for the afternoon fishing. As I had worked hard all morning, I made up my mind that as far as the afternoon fishing was concerned, I was going to do it *à la* England, "fish the rise." The only trouble was that after watching the stretch I intended to fish, there was no apparent rise to work to.

There were fewer flies emerging than there had been in the morning, but as far as could be seen fish were not the least bit interested in them. This was hard to understand, because I had not been out of sight of the stream since early morning and felt quite positive that trout had not yet done any surface feeding, nor had we been able to move any on nymphs.

After carefully watching the stream for about fifteen minutes, I thought I saw a flash of gold, very close to shore in a shallow run, but I was sure that there had been no "break." I watched the spot carefully, and in a few moments again believed I saw the flash of color, but this time I was positive that there had been no splash, and although the current was rather fast at that point, I felt certain that had there been one, I would have seen it.

I just about made up my mind that it was a trout "nymphing" when I saw a March Brown floating down toward the spot where I had seen the activity. The next thing I knew, it simply disappeared, having been "sucked in," in very much the same manner that large fish feed. Because the water was so shallow at that point, I was reasonably sure that it was not a big trout, and supposed that it was an undersized fish. At least it was action, so I cast over the fish.

My fly floated over the fish, and it too disappeared in exactly the same manner as had the natural. To my surprise I was into a fish slightly better than a foot in length, which was fully twice as long as I had expected it would be, in such shallow water, so close to shore. It was certainly not the kind of place I would expect to find a decent fish.

Taking my cue from this, I worked upstream, fishing the spots close to shore, and paying no attention to the water that I would normally expect to fish. I wound up the afternoon by catching forty-seven trout, twenty-eight browns and nineteen rainbows, ranging in size from eight to fifteen inches. As we wanted a few to eat, I kept the six largest.

Apparently the fish had realized that the few flies emerging were not getting out into the stream, so they simply took their food where they found it. Why the trout passed up the flies in the morning that were passing over them in their regular hiding places, and then moved into a strange part of the stream to feed, is another of those mysteries of trout fishing.

I was anxious to know how my companions had fared, and hoped that they had made the same discovery. When we got together I found they had moved very few fish, and I knew they thought I was handing them a line when I told them of my experience, despite the fact that I had six decent fish to show.

On the following day fish worked in exactly the same manner, so they realized I had not been kidding them the day before, and we all took some nice fish.

In talking over this unusual condition and trying to determine the reason, one of my friends offered the thought that possibly here was an instance where the "Solunar theory" had hit it right. None of us agreed with this idea, but we did not have one of the books showing the major feeding periods. However, one of the boys at the inn had one, so we checked up on it when we returned.

We did not find our answer there, because neither the major nor minor periods were even close to the time we caught our fish.

The thing that made it doubly hard to understand was the manner in which fish were taking flies these two days, with no fuss whatsoever. As a rule, when trout feed on March Browns they do some very "splashy" feeding, owing no doubt to the way the fly acts, rising from and dropping back to the surface of the stream.

The dressing for the American March Brown

NATURAL and ARTIFICIAL FLIES
in COLOR

photographs by DOUG SWISHER *and* CARL RICHARDS

Iron fraudator

QUILL GORDON

For easy identification, the photographs are
somewhat larger than life size; the approximate
sizes of the naturals are given in the chart on the
last pages of this book.
All artificials were tied by Art Flick.

Ephemerella subvaria (F)

HENDRICKSON

Ephemerella subvaria (M)

RED QUILL

Stenonema vicarium

MARCH BROWN

Stenonema fuscum

GREY FOX

Stenonema canadensis

LIGHT CAHILL

Ephemera guttulata

GREY FOX VARIANT

Ephemerella attenuata

SMALL DUN VARIANT

Isonychia bicolor

DUN VARIANT

Potamanthus distinctus

CREAM VARIANT

was originated by Mr. Preston Jennings, and it is one of the most killing flies that it has been my pleasure to use. Mr. Jennings' dressing is as follows:

> Wings—flank feather of mallard drake
> Body—red fox belly mixed with sandy poll from a hare's ear
> Hackle—bright red game cock, with a gray grizzle cock's hackle worked in as the front hackle
> Tail—red game cock's barbs
> Hook—No. 9 Hardy
> Silk—orange

In tying this fly, I make it a bit different than the original, but it is definitely a copy of it. There probably is not sufficient difference between the two to amount to anything. While I was trying to decide which of the two was better, it so happened that I took a few more fish on the artificial dressed a bit differently, but I certainly would not go so far as to say it is a better fly, and due credit should go to Mr. Jennings for its introduction.

My dressing for the American March Brown follows:

> Wings—flank feather from mandarin drake with distinct brownish cast and heavier bars

Body—light fawn-colored fur from red fox

Hackle—dark grizzly, with dark ginger grizzly wound over it, so that the two hackles are blended together

Tail—ginger cock's barbs

Hook—No. 10 or 12

Silk—orange

8

GREY FOX

(Stenonema Fuscum)

S. FUSCUM IS the second fly in the *Stenonema* group to appear on our streams, and is almost as important as *vicarium*. It usually starts emerging a few days after *S. vicarium* has been on the water, so that very often both flies are found at the same time.

It is very similar in appearance, although a bit smaller and much lighter in color. The wings of the Grey Fox do not slant back quite as decidedly as those of the March Brown. It has the brown leg markings characteristic of the group.

The habits of both the nymphs and flies are identical to those of the March Brown, and it has been my experience that fish are not the least bit selective between the two. I can find no record in my notes of trout taking the one artificial when refusing the other if both naturals were present.

It is possible that on some streams only one of the species is found, although no such report has ever reached me.

Some fishermen seem to prefer the Grey Fox artificial to that of the March Brown, but as nearly as I can determine, this is strictly a personal preference of the one using the fly.

In order to check on this, I have often fished with one fly and then the other, changing back and forth, but I am still no more partial to one than the other when both flies are on the water. I have found, though, that the fish will take the March Brown better before the Grey Fox natural appears on the water, the same as they prefer the Grey Fox after the March Brown hatch is over.

The Grey Fox was also originated by Mr. Preston Jennings. The dressing of it follows:

> Wings—flank feather of a mallard drake
> Body—light fawn-colored fur from red fox
> Hackle—light grizzly wound over light ginger
> Tail—ginger cock's barbs
> Hook—No. 12
> Silk—primrose

Tied in sizes 14 and 16, the Grey Fox is an extremely effective fly even when the hatch is over, later in the season.

9

LIGHT CAHILL

(Stenonema Canadensis)

THE THIRD FLY in this group that interests us is *Stenonema canadensis,* which is represented by that well-known dry fly the Light Cahill.

It is doubtful if any fly compares with it in popularity, especially in the East, and it is probably one dry fly that all fishermen carry. This popularity is well earned, and it is probable that more fish have been taken on this than on any other pattern of dry fly.

To date I have never met a fisherman who had fished any stream where trout could not be taken on this fly, so it probably has the distinction of being one of the few things that fishermen agree upon.

The natural usually emerges late in the afternoon and early evening, but on cloudy days I have seen it on the stream in the morning.

Because they normally start emerging around the latter part of May or first of June, they may appear on some streams only late in the evening. Often at this time of the year certain streams, owing to lack of shade or other conditions, may be rather warm. On such waters the fly will not appear until the stream has cooled off a bit, after the sun is down.

The natural has most of the characteristics of this group, but is smaller than either *vicarium* or *fuscum*. It is also lighter in color, being a pale yellow with mottled wings, the marking not as pronounced as in *S. vicarium* and *S. fuscum*. It also has wings that slant back, and the typical brown markings on the legs.

As nearly as I can determine, the artificial of this fly was originated by Theodore Gordon, but the *present* method of dressing the Light Cahill was first used by Mr. William Chandler of Neversink, New York, and it is quite different from the old Cahill that was popular for so many years.

Although it is probably known to all dry-fly fishermen, the dressing for the Light Cahill follows:

Wings—flank feather of mandarin or wood-
   duck drake
Body—light belly fur of red fox
Hackle—very light ginger cock
Tail—ginger cock's barbs
Hook—No. 12 or 14
Silk—yellow

Most fly-tyers seem to prefer this pattern
when tied on a No. 14 hook, but usually I have
found it equally effective when represented by a
size 12.

Another artificial that is probably tied to
imitate *S. canadensis* is known as the Red Fox.
This fly is so similar to the Light Cahill that I can
see no necessity for the distinction in the two flies,
and I believe that the Light Cahill will take fish at
any time the Red Fox will.

There are several other flies in the *Stenonema* group, but none of them seem to be important
from a fishing standpoint, because the flies emerge
after dark.

10

GREEN DRAKE

(Ephemera Guttulata)

Ephemera guttulata. ♀ Subimago.

I DOUBT IF any May fly that appears on most streams is as well known to trout fishermen as the Green Drake, for it is outstanding in many respects.

It is the largest May fly we have, excepting those that live in lakes or very slow-moving streams and rivers, and it seems to occur in the greatest portion of our important trout streams.

On some streams there are not many of them, whereas on others they are extremely abundant, coming literally in swarms.

Strangely enough, it is *the* fly on some waters, and is the one for which many fishermen wait with the greatest degree of hope and expectation. In other sections it is just another fly, and one that would not be missed by the fishermen.

On the Brodhead Creek in Pennsylvania, I am told by angling friends, it is by far the most important fly of the entire season, and when it is on the water all the really big fish in the stream come to life. Fish will rise to this fly that will disregard surface food at any other time during the day. It is not hard to understand this, because the Green Drake is so large that even a big trout does not need so very many of them to have a pretty good meal. I have some whose bodies measure one inch in length, although the average is somewhat smaller.

Since they are so large and heavy, it takes the naturals a long time to get off the surface, so that trout can look them over very carefully.

They have the same habit as *S. vicarium* and *S. fuscum,* making many unsuccessful attempts to fly. If anything the Green Drake takes still longer, for the wings seem out of all proportion to the heavy body.

This commotion in still waters is hard for even the biggest trout to resist, and it gives the dry-fly fisherman a fair chance to tangle with large fish that he may not be able to raise at any other time during the entire season.

On a stream where I have spent most of my time the past few years the Green Drake is relatively unimportant, and it comes and goes without our giving it much attention. I for one would never miss it.

Many trout fishermen who think of the Green Drake as the big event of the season may doubt the truth of that statement, but the reason for it is rather obvious and easy to understand.

On this water the Green Drake comes at almost the same time as the March Brown and Grey Fox, as will be noted in the three-years' record of emergence.

Whereas the March Brown and the Grey Fox are sporadic emergers and are on the water a big share of the day, the Green Drake does not show up until later in the day. Usually by the time it has started to emerge the fish have already fed on the *Stenonema* nymphs or duns. They therefore do not bother much with the Green Drakes.

On the other hand, if the fish do not feed until late in the day, because there are always more March Browns and Grey Fox on the water than Green Drakes, they are not the least bit selective, and will take one as readily as the other.

As far as my own likes on the matter are concerned, this condition suits me very well, for I have yet to see a really good artificial of the Green Drake that will take fish consistently. All will take some fish, especially little fellows, but they are not what I consider consistently good flies.

The reason for this is not difficult to understand. The natural size of this fly is such that the artificial must be large, and obviously the larger the dry fly, the easier it is for trout to discern its artificiality. This is especially true with fish that feed in the still waters.

So far the most effective fly that I have found to fool large trout feeding on natural Green Drakes is a very large Grey Fox Variant that has been well tied with good stiff hackles. Many of my friends have also found this fly productive with reasonable consistency, more so than other artificials.

Here is the dressing for the Grey Fox Variant:

Wings—none
Body—quill from either light ginger or cream cock's hackle
Hackles *—one light ginger, one dark ginger, one grizzly cock's hackle
Tail—ginger cock's barbs
Hook—No. 10 or 12
Silk—primrose

---

* When the hackles are wound, one should be wound over the other and they should be bunched as much as possible.

If all streams were like the last one mentioned, it would be a tremendous disappointment to many dry-fly fishermen. I know a number who are fortunate enough to be able to take their vacations at any time they choose, on just a few minutes' notice. They seem to live from one year to the next, just waiting for the word that the Green Drake is on the water—very much like those who await word from Maine that "The Ice Is Out."

Year after year, these enthusiasts will be found on their pet streams, feeling that this will be the year they will catch the "big one of their dreams" on a dry fly. Even if the fly does not materialize, they have the fun of thinking about it.

Just the fact that big fish will rise when the Green Drake is emerging seems to make many fishermen get as excited as a kid on the last day of school.

Generally, this species does not appear on the stream for as long a period as the other May flies. The main hatches seldom last more than ten days, and more often about a week. Individuals may of course be found for some time after the main hatches are over, sometimes stringing along for as much as two weeks.

The spinner of the Green Drake is as familiar to most fishermen as the dun, and is known as the Coffin Fly. Very few fishermen seem to realize that there is any connection between the two, however, so this bit of information may come as a surprise to them.

There is such a difference in the appearance of the two flies that it is hard to connect them, but you cannot have Coffin Flies without first having Green Drakes. It is hard to believe that a fly with a decidedly green wing and heavy yellowish body with brown markings and comparatively short tails can turn into a fly with clear, glossy wings with black markings, a slender waxy-white body, and very long tails. Nevertheless, such is the case. The derivation of the Coffin Fly's name is obvious, from its appearance.

The imitation of this spinner is also one that in most cases has not been too successful. Although I am possibly a bit prejudiced, I have never found any that I like as well as an imitation I tied a few years ago, but it is still far from good.

My dressing for the Coffin Fly follows:

Wings—flank feather from mallard drake
Body—white quill from a porcupine (must be well soaked)
Hackle—very light natural dun
Tail—three black rabbit whiskers
Hook—No. 10
Silk—olive

The spinners return to the stream late in the evening, just before dark, and it is quite a sight to see these white specks darting around in the air. They are very fast flyers and difficult to catch, just the opposite of the dun, which is slow and lumbering and has difficulty in flying.

The female spinner does not drop off her eggs, like the female of *E. subvaria,* but dips them off, touching the end of her body to the surface of the water. It is at this time that fish feed on the Coffin Fly. The male can readily be identified by the longer tails and the forceps at the end of the body.

11

DUN VARIANT

(Isonychia Bicolor)

Isonychia bicolor ♂ subimago.

THIS MAY FLY should be easy for all fishermen to recognize because of one characteristic. It is the only fly of importance to us whose legs differ in color.

In *Isonychia,* the forelegs are brown and the other two sets of legs are light yellow, which accounts for the fly's name, *bicolor*. It has a very dark dun wing, in some cases almost black, and the body is a reddish brown and is quite long.

Another trait of this splendid fly is the manner in which it carries its forelegs when at rest, holding them out, parallel with and ahead of the body.

The fly itself is larger than either the March Brown or Grey Fox, but not quite so large as the Green Drake.

For some reason, Mother Nature seems to favor this May fly over all others, in more ways than one. Unlike other flies, when water conditions are normal the nymph does not rise to the surface where the fly emerges, nor does the perfect insect emerge below the water as is the case with the *Iron* family.

Instead, the *Isonychia* nymph swims to shallow water along shore, quite some time before the fly is ready to come out, and when the emergence period arrives, the nymph leaves the stone under which it has been hiding, crawls up on it, well above the surface of the water, and there the fly hatches, out of reach of fish. It can take its sweet time drying its wings, with nothing to worry about until it flies away. An exception to this is when the water is high, at which time the fly seems to emerge in the stream.

The nymph also has an advantage over those of other species in that it is one of the fastest swimmers of all, and when in the water is very difficult to catch. Trout, of course, do not experience so much trouble in catching them, although fewer are taken in normal water by fish than other species.

Owing to their habit of emerging on dry land, not so many of the flies get to the stream, unless the weather happens to be rainy or there is a lot of wind, and then it is seldom that trout pass them up when they float over them.

It has been my experience that rainbow trout are very partial to this May fly, and some of the finest fishing I have ever enjoyed was when this fly was on the water. Even in good weather, when there is neither rain nor wind to help us, there always seems to be a fair number of cripples that find their way to the stream. When this insect gets on the water it seems to realize that it should not be there, and tries doubly hard to fly off, its wings going most of the time. This trait makes it very attractive to trout, and it is usually taken in a hurry.

Although it is unimportant, there is one thing about this fly that has always interested me. As a rule, several flies will emerge on the same rock, and all of the nymphs seem to crawl to the same height on the stone, so that the cases form a straight line after the flies have emerged. Yet right alongside there will be another rock with not a single *Isonychia* case on it. This sight must be familiar to all fishermen who are the least bit observant.

This fly usually emerges in the evening, but will be found in the daytime in large numbers when the streams are unusually high or discolored.

In most streams it appears on more days than any other May fly. In my collection record for the third year, it will be noted that *Isonychia* was found in May, June, July and August. It is therefore a fly of the greatest importance to the fly fisherman, as well as being an important item in the trout's diet.

If you are fortunate enough to run into this fly when it is emerging during the day, you will more than likely experience some of the darndest fishing you have ever seen. For some unknown reason, when feeding on this fly in the daytime trout lose all of their usual timidity, and often it is next to impossible to "put them down." They will often take almost any fly offered, regardless of size or color.

I will never forget one afternoon a few years ago, when fish were gorging themselves on *Isonychias*.

I happened to be instructing a beginner, who had done quite a bit of reading about fishing with the dry fly but who had no experience in actual fishing. I thought my pupil was going to have a heart attack, for it made no difference how his fly was presented, there was always a fish waiting to take it. Drag meant nothing, and even when his fly hit the water hard enough to scare every fish in the stream, he still took trout. The fact that he was in such a hurry to get his fly back onto the water resulted in his losing four out of five that he hooked, and he was just like a crazy man.

When it was all over he said to me, "Well, it certainly did not take me long to get onto dry-fly fishing, did it? From what I had read, I thought it would take quite a bit of practice." I might add that he has since found out that he was a bit premature in his statement.

That evening, when the gang got together, it was found that all of us had experienced the same kind of fishing that afternoon. As one fisherman expressed it, "I threw everything over them but the kitchen sink, and took fish right along." Another angler reported that he had deliberately walked up the center of the stream where some fish were feeding, to see if it would bother them, and within less than a minute they were rising as regularly as they had been before.

It is the kind of day you read about but seldom see, and certainly one to add to our store of memories.

Because it is a large fly, *Isonychia* is rather difficult to imitate, as in the case of the Green Drake. A large Red Quill, tied on a No. 10 hook with very dark dun hackles and black hackle point wings, makes a good imitation, but I prefer a variant of this fly, as I have found it much more satisfactory in every respect. It is called the Dun Variant, and is one of the most killing patterns that I have ever fished with.

I have never known it to fail when *Isonychias*

were on the water, and have taken some of the largest trout on it that I have ever caught on a dry fly. I prefer it to a Red Quill, tied on the larger hook because it rides high, making it easier to see, floats much better, and will take a lot more punishment than the winged fly. Another point in its favor is the speed with which you can get it ready to fish, after having caught a trout. A swish in the water to clean it, a few false casts, and it is all ready for action. A well-tied variant requires no oil to make it float.

The dressing for the Dun Variant follows:

Wings—none
Body—few turns of quill from Rhode Island Red cock's hackle, well soaked
Hackle—natural dark dun, either large regular, spade, or saddle hackles
Tail—dun barb or spades, very long
Hook—No. 12, short shank
Silk—olive

The spinner of *Isonychia* is very similar to the dun, except of course that it has the clear wings and longer tails that are characteristic of spinners. The legs are the same, and the body is a bit more reddish that that of the dun.

They return to the stream in large numbers,

and the fish seem to feed on them whenever they get the chance, as readily as they do the duns. This may be due to the fact that both the duns and spinners are apt to be on the stream at the same time, and they may mistake one for the other.

Very often the spinners are active after the hatch is over, and many that are spent will float down to the still waters from the riffles above. Here again the Dun Variant will work very well, and will take fish that are feeding on the spent flies.

If you happen to locate any large rainbows I would suggest that you try for them with a Dun Variant when *Isonychia* is on the water. Unless I am greatly mistaken, you will raise them without much difficulty, if they are the least bit interested in surface food. It is one of the best flies for rainbow trout that I know of.

12

BLUE-WINGED OLIVE

(Ephemerella Attenuata)

THIS VERY IMPORTANT fly was left out of the original STREAMSIDE GUIDE because we could not get it identified. Apparently Dr. Spieth, who did the identification work for me, did not recognize this one, so he did not include it in the collecting records. It was present in good numbers all of the years I was collecting and is an important item of food for trout, coming as it does in such great numbers in a normal year. It is equally important to fishermen, since the fish are so active when the fly is emerging. The name is self-explanatory for purposes of identification, for when it emerges, it has a distinct olive body, with very dark dun wings. As the insect is exposed to the air, the bright olive color changes to a darker shade.

When Let Thompson was drawing both the nymphs and flies, he was annoyed that he could not get the species identified. I gathered many of the nymphs for him and he kept them in an aquarium covered by a screened cage, which enabled him to draw the nymph, sub-imago, and imago from life.

In a last-ditch effort to get the information we wanted, he wrote Dr. J. Traver, who was the "May fly expert of the day," feeling she would certainly come up with its name. When her reply arrived, we about died, for she told him that the only way she could make a positive identification was for us to furnish her with a *"virgin* male imago." We got quite a kick out of that, for we were not about to post a guard to watch the aquarium in its screened cage for twenty-four hours a day to make sure there was no hanky-panky. Like the Quill Gordon, this fly emerges under water and trout seem to feed on it mostly just as it reaches the surface, after having shed its shuck, with the wings still closed.

On several occasions when examining the stomach contents of trout over two pounds, we have found *attenuata* nymphs, which are somewhat of a dirty brown, in the lower part; on top of them, the freshly emerged flies, with the wings still folded, the bodies an extremely bright olive; and then on the third layer, some of the flies after they had opened their wings, the bodies slightly darker. In every case, it appeared that the trout had started feeding on the nymphs, then a large number of freshly emerged flies, and last a few of the fully developed flies.

A wet fly has worked well for me on occasion, as has a dry fly, if one is lucky enough to hit the fish when they are really taking them on top, as they will at times.

The dressing for a fly that I have found effective follows:

Wings—none

Body—mixture of pulled-apart olive yarn, with a small amount of muskrat fur blended with it; body should be very small and should not contain enough fur to overcome the olive cast

Hackle—natural dark dun

Tail—dark dun, very sparse

Hook—No. 16 or 18

Silk—olive

This fly is actually a small Dun Variant, but with an olive body.

13

CREAM VARIANT

(Potamanthus Distinctus)

THIS IS THE last large May fly to appear on most trout waters, and although it does not occur in all streams, it is felt to be of sufficient importance to include in this book.

It has several local names, such as Evening Dun, Cream Dun, Golden Dun, and Pale Evening Dun, and one name fits it as well as the other.

It is a very easy fly to identify, being large, just a bit smaller than *Isonychia,* but its color is very light. On some streams it is cream-colored and on others has a very faint yellow tinge, both body and wings being the same shade. The tails are three in number and are comparatively short for the length of the fly's body.

Normally it emerges in the evening, in the still waters. The habits of the nymph are similar to those of the Green Drake.

Unlike most May flies found in streams that harbor trout, *Potamanthus* does not seem to be adversely affected by high water temperatures, and I have found this fly emerging when the water was nearly eighty.

On cloudy days the fly will often appear during the late afternoon, and on some streams that I have reports on it apparently emerges as often in the afternoon as it does in the evening. Such has not been my experience, though, and except on cloudy days, I have always found it emerging late in the evening.

This fly is well imitated by a Cream Variant, and it is one that can be used as well for evening fishing throughout the latter part of the season, when trout do almost all of their surface feeding. Of course, it is more easily seen than most flies late in the evening.

Another fly that emerges at the same time is *Ephemera varia,* a cousin of the Green Drake. It is so similar to *Potamanthus* that it is often mistaken for it.

The dressing of the Cream Variant follows:

Wings—none

Body—quill from hackle of cream or white
cock, well soaked
Hackles—large cream regular, saddle, or
spade (not those with black centers)
Hook—No. 12, short shank
Tails—cream cock's barbs, long
Silk—yellow

14

STONE FLIES

ALTHOUGH THE PURPOSE of this book is more to correlate dry flies, and in some cases nymphs, with the natural May flies, there are two stone flies I believe worthy of mention. Because I have had such good luck with the artificials that represent them, I feel they should be listed here. Both are of value to us when we can do little with dry flies, and are the most effective early in the season, before May flies have started to emerge.

Immediately preceding the first May flies, the Early Brown Stone is found very early in the spring on most streams. It is important to fishermen because it seems to be the first aquatic insect in which trout show a real interest.

Fish will occasionally take it on the surface, but more often than not take it underwater. It is one of the very large family of stone flies, and coming as early in the season as it does, it is not apt to be mistaken for any other fly. The fly has a reddish brown body with dun-colored wings that fold flat over the body when the fly is at rest.

The name "Early Brown Stone" fits this insect perfectly, and to the best of my knowledge the fly was given this name by Preston Jennings. The proper name is *Taeniopteryx fasciata,* which is an awful "handle" to put on such an inoffensive little insect.

Although it is small, the fish seem very fond of it, and as a rule they feed heavily on them. I have found trout early in the season that were literally stuffed with them. There does not seem to be any special emergence time and they are apt to be found at any time of the day, but as a rule sometime in the afternoon.

The dressing for the Early Brown Stone follows:

Wings—two small dun hackle points tied flat over body

Body—quill from Rhode Island Red cock's hackle

Hackle—soft blue dun hen's hackle

Tail—none necessary

Hook—No. 14

Silk—olive

This fly is of course fished wet.

The other stone fly that I have found well worth imitating is the creeper of *Perla capitata,* an insect that most fishermen are familiar with.

Although this fly does not emerge until the end of June or first of July, trout feed on the creepers during the entire season and take them whenever they have an opportunity.

They spend all of their nymphal stage under stones in the riffles, but in spite of this they are very poor swimmers, apparently having great difficulty getting back to the bottom of the stream if they happen to get into the current.

During periods of high water in the spring large quantities of them are washed into the stream, at which time trout have a grand feast.

As this is usually the time that trout fishermen are forced to use bucktails or bait, these imitations are a valuable addition, and I have had some very fine fishing with them.

Trout take the stone-fly creeper best when the water is a bit high, preferably not roily. It should be fished across and downstream. During periods of high water it seems to work equally as well in pools or riffles, and fish as a rule hit it very hard.

For those of you who are more ambitious than I, and like to fish at dawn, I suggest that you try this lure in the pocket water and fast runs during July. The fly emerges during the night, right up to daylight, and some nice fish will be taken on the imitation of the creeper at that time.

When the fly is ready to emerge, the creeper leaves the stream and crawls up on a stone, where the nymph case opens. The sight of these empty cases must be familiar to most fishermen. They are usually on stones in rather fast water.

The dressing of the stone-fly creeper follows:

Body—large quill from light ginger cock's
    hackle, and seal's fur dyed amber
Wing case—wide barred flank feather from
    mandarin drake or wood duck, tied flat
    extending full length of body
Legs—grouse hackle
Tail—two barbs from cock pheasant's tail;
    should be at least one-half inch long
Hook—No. 8
Silk—primrose

In the tying of this creeper, there should be a slight hump made on the hook, but not large as in the Hendrickson or March Brown nymphs.

In the forming of the body, the quill should be put on first, starting at the tail and going almost to the hump. Then the seal fur should be wound, extending almost to the eye of the hook.

The mandarin or wood-duck feather should be fastened exactly the same as in the other nymphs, except that it extends to the *end* of the body, and is not cut off short, next to the hump.

No ribbing is necessary in this fly.

15

NYMPHS

EVEN THOUGH NYMPHS are much more important in a trout's diet than are the mature flies or spinners, very few fishermen have either the time or inclination to study them. Because more and more people are evincing an interest in them every year, it was felt an addition, touching briefly on these interesting creatures, would add value to STREAMSIDE GUIDE. It is not expected that the average fisherman is really going to make a study of them, nor is that really necessary; but knowing something of their habits enables the angler to know why imitations of some are really valuable, whereas others are almost worthless.

All nymph imitations will undoubtedly take fish at certain times, and some are really outstanding. I know some fishermen who are experts with them, and they take some fine fish when the dry-fly fisherman can do very little.

There is one thing that is sadly lacking in most of these nymphs. In the majority of cases even the originator cannot tell the species of fly they are supposed to imitate. This is particularly true with reference to those that are supposed to represent May flies.

As a rule, it is just some "bug" that was found under a stone, or taken from a trout's stomach, and an artificial was tied to look something like it.

Usually when fishermen buy these lures, they forget they have them until sometime when they are fishing and can do nothing with their old favorites. Then they remember their new nymph and decide to try it out.

If it happens that they have no luck on it, back it goes into the box, often with some undeserved remarks. On the other hand, if it happens to produce a few trout, it is fished with confidence, and the fisherman gets more proficient in its use.

For the past few years I have been experimenting with this subject, and although I have made some headway, there is still a lot to learn about it. Because it is a known fact that nymphs are the most active just prior to the time that the fly emerges, I believed that imitations of them at that period would be the most valuable from a fishing standpoint. It is at that time they leave their hiding places, and they seem to lose their natural caution.

In these experiments it was of course first necessary to learn which nymphs spent their lives in the riffles and which in the silt. Those living in the silt at the bottom of pools were less valuable to us than the others, because when the nymphs of these species got into the stream proper it was in more or less still water, a place where trout had plenty of opportunity to look them over. As they are the largest of the nymphs, it is difficult to make really good imitations that will fool trout.

On the other hand, those that emerge in faster water are smaller, and fish cannot afford to take so much time, having either to take or leave them.

The next step was to correlate the May fly and nymph. After this was learned, and the results checked and double checked, came the job of making imitations that were practical, not too expensive, and good fish takers. To make an exact representation was a pretty expensive proposition, and the result was lures that were too costly for the average fisherman.

Then followed a long process of trial and error, which with the greatly appreciated help of friends resulted in some that were quite effective, when used at the proper time.

The artificials described later are some that I have had good luck with, when used at the time the corresponding fly is hatching. For example, if you know that the Hendrickson is the fly that is emerging, and that it can be expected at about two P.M., you also know that the nymph will be active for some time before, so the artificial is fished from say one P.M. until the flies start to appear.

These nymphs have special appeal to the dry-fly fisherman, for exactly the same tackle is used as for dry flies, excepting the fly, of course, and they are used at a time when dry-fly fishing is apt to be unproductive.

One thing that impressed me particularly was the way that fish will hit these nymphs, smashing them as hard as they do bucktails.

Very often when fishing them on a leader with a 3X tippet, I have been caught asleep and had the fish snap the leader when it took the nymph, because my rod tip was not raised sufficiently. However, most works on the subject by other writers speak of the manner in which trout take them as very light. Some even advise attaching a large dry fly to the leader above the nymph, so that the fact that a trout had struck would be known.

It is my belief that the chief reason for the difference in my experience is that when I fish these artificials, it is the natural time for fish to take them, there being many nymphs present at the time.

Please bear in mind that these imitations are no better than any other artificial nymph, when fished any time other than when the corresponding May fly is due to hatch.

Thanks to these nymphs, many a dull hour on the stream has been turned into a profitable one. They are not difficult to make and will take a lot of abuse. Many minutes that might otherwise be spent sitting on the bank can be turned into more pleasant ones, while waiting for the hatch.

When March Browns, Grey Foxes, and Cahills are emerging, since they come more or less all day, a few at a time, much good fishing can be had with March Brown nymphs. Use them as you would a dry fly, fishing a floating line, casting upstream exactly as you would a dry. The nymph will of course sink, and when a fish strikes, it will show on the floating line. In this type of fishing, it is necessary to watch your line even more carefully than you would a dry fly, striking gently at the moment you see the line move.

This manner of nymph fishing is necessary only when the trout are not "on the feed," but it will produce some nice fish.

♀ Iron fraudator
Quill Gordon

QUILL GORDON

This fly, as well as others in the *Iron* group, has one peculiarity. Unlike most other May flies, this one actually leaves its shuck under water, and swims to the surface with its wings not fully developed. To my knowledge, no other important May fly, other than *E. attenuata,* does this.

There is no point in trying to imitate the nymph because of this trait. It lives under stones in the riffles, and does not show itself to any extent until it is nearly ready to emerge. A few days before emergence time, large numbers of them (as well as those of *E. subvaria*) will be seen clinging to the downstream sides of the stones. When "E-Day" arrives, the case splits open and out pops the fly. Many of these flies fail to reach the surface and instead are carried downstream to the waiting mouth of a trout. This is probably the reason the Quill Gordon wet fly is so successful.

Although of no importance to fishermen, except to help identify it, the nymph of the Quill

Gordon is the only one of importance having only two tails. All others have three. My dressing for the wet Quill Gordon follows:

> Wings—flank feather of mandarin or wood
>   duck tied flat on back
> Body—same as dry fly
> Hackle—natural blue dun hen
> Tail—mandarin flank feather
> Hook—No. 12

HENDRICKSON

♀ *Ephemerella subvaria*
Hendrickson

The nymph of *E. subvaria* is of considerable importance to fishermen. Owing to its habits, it affords good fishing for about a half hour prior to the actual hatch. On occasion, fish can also be taken on an imitation of these nymphs after they have stopped feeding on the surface.

When the time nears for the fly to emerge, the nymph becomes restless and will often rise to the surface and drop back to the stream bottom, doing this several times before it makes its last trip to the surface. It then floats for quite some distance, trying all the while to break open its case. It is at this time that fish feed on them, and they continue to do so until the flies start to emerge.

The dressing for the Hendrickson nymph follows:

> Body—blend of grey fox belly fur, beaver, and claret seal, worked together until material is of a greyish-brown shade
> Wing case—bit of blue heron wing
> Legs—partridge hackle
> Tail—mandarin flank feather
> Rib—tying silk, or fine gold wire
> Hook—No. 12
> Silk—olive

Instructions for tying are as follows:
Make a slight hump on the hook, near the eye, with yarn or other material. Fasten in the tail and start winding the body, the fur being loosely spun, going over the hump. Tie in, just back of the eye of the hook. Fasten in heron feather about one sixteenth of an inch in width, to represent wing case, then wind hackle, and finish off the

head. Go back to the tail and start winding either the tying silk or gold wire toward hump, to represent the segments of the nymph's body, going as far as the hump. Then tie in the other end of the wing case, which should be cut off short, where tied in. Lacquer the wing case, as well as the head of the nymph.

As mentioned previously, this does not even approximately resemble the appearance of the natural nymph, but it must suggest it to the trout, which is more important.

There is another May fly that comes on the water after dark, and although it is of no value to the fly fisherman, the trout feed on its nymphs before dark. When fish are feeding on them, fishermen are apt to think that they are working on the surface, and lose a lot of time trying to take them on dry flies. Instead they are "tailing," and at such times the same dressing for the Hendrickson nymph on a size 16 hook will produce some nice fish that might otherwise not be taken.

PALE EVENING DUN

Another of the very important *Ephemerella* group, this nymph is very active late in the day and trout feed on them with gusto. Apparently they take it just as it reaches the surface; more often than not, a fisherman will swear the fish are surface feeding on flies, whereas they are actually taking the nymphs just as they are ready to emerge on top, after drifting. With careful observation, it will be noted that the duns in the main are floating untouched, but rises will be seen where no fly is apparent.

The same nymph as made to imitate the Hendrickson works well, but tied on a No. 16 or 18 hook.

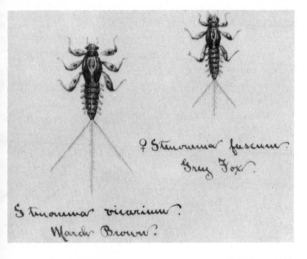

MARCH BROWN   **GREY FOX**

CAHILL

In appearance, the nymphs of these three flies are very similar, except for the size. It has been my experience that the March Brown nymph is almost as important to fishermen as that of the Hendrickson. Actually, it is a toss-up as to which has been more important in taking fish.

Although all three are in the *Stenonema* family, the nymph of the March Brown seems to be more attractive to trout, probably due to its method of emergence. As mentioned previously, just prior to being ripe, the nymph swims or crawls to shallow water and when ready to emerge, swims to the surface, wiggling to free itself of its case. This commotion attracts fish, and not being a fast swimmer, many are taken on their way up, which no doubt accounts for the effectiveness of the artificial.

Apparently, neither the Grey Fox nor the Cahill "mess around" this way, but instead swim to the surface and emerge much faster, although the same imitations tied to imitate the March Brown are effective (to a lesser degree) tied on No. 12 and 14 hooks.

The dressing for the March Brown nymph follows:

> Body—seal fur, dyed amber, mixed with a small amount of fawn-colored fur from red fox belly
>
> Wing case—from short tail of cock pheasant, underside to be on topside of nymph

Legs—partridge hackle

Tail—three strands from a cock pheasant's
longest tail feather

Ribbing—single strand brown embroidery
cotton

Hook—No. 10

The instructions for tying this nymph are
identical to those for making the Hendrickson
nymph.

GREEN DRAKE

♀ Ephemera guttulata.
Green Drake.

The nymph of this fly really "bugged" me.
Everything I'd read said they live in the silt,
mostly at the tails of pools, and I was perfectly
willing to believe it since some of the writers were

famed entomologists, whereas I was just an interested fisherman. However, much as I dug in the silt, the only large nymphs I could come up with were those of *P. distinctus,* or *E. varia,* a fly in the same family as the Green Drake. In confirmation, it looked the same as the empty cases I'd seen of *E. guttulata,* except that it was smaller and thinner. Never did I find the one I wanted.

One day, my good friend Let Thompson, the artist who did the drawings of the nymphs, said he was sick of this business of not being able to procure a live nymph, or at least one in solution, and that he would offer me 50 cents cash if I'd produce one for him. He wanted to draw one "from life."

That did it. I made a large net of cheese cloth, fifteen feet long with two long sticks at the ends. I felt that when the flies were emerging, by holding the net across fifteen feet of stream, I would surely get some live ones as they drifted into it. This presented the problem of needing help and my narrow-minded fishing pals were somewhat reluctant to give up fishing time to help me try to catch some damned bugs. A couple finally weakened, but instead of getting nymphs I got "shook up."

We ran the net across and waited a few minutes. Flies were emerging a few feet ahead of us, but all we managed to get were empty cases, so we assumed we were too far down. Every time we moved upstream, though, the emerging flies were taking off ahead of us. After drawing a complete blank, we knew the nymphs were not drifting, nor were they only emerging at the tail of the pool, for we found them in every part of it.

Finally, I decided to "make like a blue heron" and stand in one spot in a fairly still part of the pool, not moving at all, just watching. It wasn't long before I saw one come from under a stone and swim to the surface, as fast as I'd ever seen a nymph swim. By careful observation, I saw others do the same thing, but when one was close enough and I made a move toward it, it swam away from me, came up, and out popped a fly. Now that the secret was out, I felt there was nothing to it, so I went to the stream bank and picked up the wide-mouth bottle containing formaldehyde. Waiting until one came up right next to me, I grabbed it fast and popped it into the bottle: I'd collected my first Green Drake nymph. The only trouble was, when I looked at my prize, I found that instead of a nymph I had a fly, not a nymph.

After several tries, with the same results, it finally dawned on me what was happening: the nymph case must have cracked before the insect started to the surface, so that it came out immediately when it hit the air. After capturing several more, I found that by gentle presure I could stop the action of emergence without crushing the nymph, as long as the pressure was applied on the thorax. So at long last, I was able to present Let with a model that he could use to draw a Green Drake nymph "from life."

Oh yes, I collected the half buck, too.

Undoubtedly its action when emerging is the reason imitations are of very little value to fishermen, for as noted, this creature swims as fast as any nymph I have ever seen—faster even than the *Isonychia* nymph—and inasmuch as it shoots right straight up, it is doubtful if fish bother much with them. And too, it may be that in the Schoharie, where the fish pay no attention to the Green Drake fly, they simply don't take the nymph either.

DUN VARIANT

♀ *Isonychia bicolor*
Lead wing.

As mentioned before, the *Isonychia* nymphs are found fairly close to shore as the emergence time for the fly nears. On many streams, fishermen have had very good luck with that well-known wet fly the Lead-Wing Coachman when this nymph is active.

Although this is an excellent fly, I like an imitation of my own concoction better, not because it is any more effective, but because it will take a lot more abuse. I do not believe that I have ever seen one of them go to pieces. The dressing for this nymph is as follows:

> Body *—dark claret seal's fur mixed with black wool that has been pulled apart
> Wing case—none
> Legs—grouse hackle
> Tail—three very short pieces of peacock herl; they should not extend beyond one eighth of an inch from the body
> Hook—No. 10
> Silk—olive

The dressing of the Lead-Wing Coachman is so well known that it is not felt necessary to give it here.

---

* No hump in the body of this nymph.

**CREAM
VARIANT**

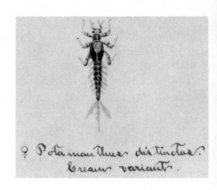

♀ Potamanthus distinctus?
cream variant.

Like the nymph of the Green Drake, this one seems to have little value, at least in the streams I fish.

It is a fast swimmer and emerges very fast, with the nymph case being cracked before it emerges. Often when collecting I have seen a nymph on the surface, but before it could be reached the fly emerged, the transformation taking only a matter of seconds.

And too, coming late in the season when the streams are on the warm side, fish don't seem to be interested in such "heavy food," preferring instead much lighter fare, if they feed at all before dark. I have not found the nymph worth imitating.

BLUE-WINGED OLIVE

♀ Ephemerella sp.
Blue-winged Olive

As noted in the May-fly section under this fly, the Blue-winged Olive emerges subsurface as does the *Iron* group.

Because careful observation proved to me that the fish feed more on the partially emerged fly than on the nymph, my efforts were spent more on an imitation of a wet fly. If I said I was completely successful, I'd not be telling the truth, although I did have fair luck with a wet fly dressed as follows:

> Wings—tips of very dark dun hackle points (black may be substituted) with just a very small amount showing; they represent the wings not completely unfolded
> Body— olive yarn
> Tail—natural dun
> Hook—No. 16 or 18
> Silk—olive

16

THE BUCKTAIL

IT HAS BEEN my expressed purpose to correlate artificials with naturals, so the same idea will be carried out with relation to bucktails.

Such being the case, the reason for leaving out the bright-colored streamers and bucktails will be quite obvious, for I doubt if anyone has ever seen a minnow or other stream inhabitant that resembles any of the flashy lures on the market.

This does not mean they are not good flies to fish with, and many are consistent in their ability to take trout.

Although trout feed on almost any minnow they can catch, there seem to be two species they are partial to. They are *Rhinichthys atratulus* and *Semotilus atromaculatus*.

They are given such local names as chubs and dace, and I have found them on every trout stream that I have fished.

Neither of them seems to attain any size, particularly *Rhinichthys atratulus,* which rarely exceeds three and a half inches in length. It is most commonly called Black-Nose Dace, and as this name is as good as any other, I will use it. Certainly it is a lot more chummy than its technical name, and a bit easier to pronounce.

Of great importance to fishermen is the appeal this little fish has to trout. In examining the stomach contents of trout over a period of many years, I have found more of them than all of the other species of minnows combined.

Both minnows travel in schools, but unlike many others, they are found in fast water as well as in pools. Unlike such minnows as Stone Cats and Cutlip Minnows, they spend very little time under stones.

Although all trout of legal size feed on minnows, they do not seem to be so important to the diet of small fish as to those having attained a length of fourteen inches or better. This, of course, is not hard to understand, because smaller fish can obtain sufficient nourishment from insect life.

As trout get larger, they need much more food than is supplied by a diet of insects alone throughout the whole season, so they turn to such food as minnows and crawfish. Very often in the season insect life is not available, and minnows at such times are the most important food.

Because the Black-Nose Dace is so well liked by trout, I tried to imitate it as closely as possible with a bucktail. The result is one that has proved itself successful, as well as one that will take a lot of abuse.

If I were much of a bucktail fisherman, my fly box would undoubtedly contain a larger number of patterns, but because I do so little of this fishing, the Black-Nose Dace is the only one I carry.

About the only time I fish it is early in the spring, and on days later in the season when I can do nothing with dry flies. Nobody realizes better than I that many hours spent in fishing with dry flies could be more profitably spent with other types of lures, but there is something about a dry fly that gets into your blood.

A good imitation of the Black-Nose Dace is very simple to tie. Having had such good luck with it, I find it hard to understand why it is not used more by fishermen. A local fisherman of my acquaintance consistently kills large fish with this lure.

Possibly its simplicity does not appeal to the eye of the fisherman, even though it does to trout. I would suggest that those of you who enjoy this kind of fishing make up a couple, or have them made by your fly-tyer. I do not think you will be without them after giving them a fair trial.

The dressing for the Black-Nose Dace follows:

Body—best quality medium silver tinsel
Tag—red yarn, very short
Hair—natural polar bear, black bear, or black hair from skunk tail, and brown bucktail
Hook—No. 4, 6, 8, or 10

After body and tag are on hook, tie in bit of natural polar-bear hair (or white bucktail) on top of hook, then a bit of black bear hair or black skunk tail on top of white, to simulate the black stripe in the minnow. Then a bit of brown bucktail on top of the black hair. I like the white and brown hair to extend about the same distance from the head, and the black just a bit shorter.

Polar-bear hair is recommended in preference to white bucktail for two reasons. After being in the water, the hair of a polar bear much more closely resembles the natural appearance of a minnow than the flat white of bucktail. And, too, in my opinion, fine polar-bear hair has a more lifelike action than bucktail.

When small-size hooks are used, such as No. 10, I suggest you try either the Chinese or Mexican deer tails. They make an excellent fly, and the hair is softer than that of the white-tail deer.

For early spring fishing, I prefer this lure on a No. 4 hook, but for later in the season, with normal water conditions, I have had better success with the smaller sizes, especially the one tied on a No. 10 hook.

For those of you who always fish bucktails downstream—that is, across stream and down—I have a suggestion to make. Later in the season, when the water gets lower, or even if it is lower than normal, try fishing these small bucktails upstream, in the pocket water.

It is not necessary to make long casts when fishing this type of water, especially if there is a lot of white water. You will find that some excellent fish can be taken on these small flies, and it makes very interesting fishing. Most trout that rise hit them hard, and the percentage of fish hooked is better than most times when bucktails are used.

Many fishermen believe bucktails are effective only in the spring when the water is high and slightly roily. Nothing could be further from the truth, and although they are best in the early part of the season, they can be fished with considerable success throughout the entire fishing season. Just as long as fish feed on minnows they are apt to take bucktails. They are extremely effective on a rising stream, particularly if the water is slightly off color.

As a matter of fact, after the main hatches of May flies are over and there is a letdown in the amount of available food, trout look for other things to take the place of flies, and minnows are usually "it."

At such times, bucktails and streamers will produce some nice fish.

Late in the season, when the water in some streams gets quite warm, the fish generally do one of two things. They either head for the spring holes or move to the fast pocket water where there is more aeration.

Bear this in mind when fishing bucktails late in the season, and look for trout where there is a good supply of oxygen. Very often in fast stretches of pocket water trout will show an interest in food, even at such times when it might be thought too warm for any kind of trout fishing.

17

SUMMER AND AUTUMN—
TERRESTRIALS AND MINUTAE

THIS IS "terrestrial and minutae" time in most of the eastern streams.

On the Schoharie, where I have done most of my fishing, due to high water temperatures we seldom have any summer fishing. And worse luck, although our season runs through September, due to low water conditions and heat, there is seldom very good fishing. Because this combination exists more often than not, my experience with late-season fishing has been very limited.

I must therefore depend more on friends' experiences than my own. Without exception, all agree that success in this fishing depends almost entirely on using sizes 20 to 24 flies. This goes for all the streams that remain cold enough in New York, Pennsylvania, and the rest of the East. The famed Battenkill, both the New York and Vermont portions, furnishes good summer fishing on the small flies. Doug Swisher, who photographed the May flies and is a terrific fisherman, has wonderful fishing on the Michigan Au Sable—but again on the minutae.

September fishing can be quite good if the stream flow is up. Because I get so much fishing, I have a bit of a guilt complex about taking fish in late September, for so often the females are not very far from their spawning run to the feeders and it has been my experience, at least, that most of the fish I get at that time of the year are females —and I'd rather they live to reproduce.

About the only May-fly imitation I've had any success with is a small, lightly dressed Red Quill from sizes 14 up, with the up sizes working best. The smaller the better.

From July through September, fish seem to like their food on the light side, the only exception being in streams that stay cool and where grasshoppers are available. Their main fare is seemingly minutae and terrestrials. May flies are almost nonexistent and from my limited experience, the only aquatic insects that trout feed on are the very young water striders, which they seem to relish, going into the shallowest water imaginable to take them. Anyone seeing this feeding for the first time would doubt the fish were trout; this of course takes place only in fairly still pools.

Vince Marinaro and Charlie Fox have done

such a superb job in their books of describing terrestrial and minutae fishing that I won't even attempt to do the job, due to my limited experience. It is so completely different from other fly fishing that it is a science all in itself.

One of my first experiences with summer fishing really shook me, since I was vain enough to think that if fish were rising I could take my share of them. My fishing pal loved dry-fly fishing as much as I do, but because of angina was limited to easy fishing in pools fairly handy to get to. That evening as we approached such a pool, it was evident that fish were really going to town, showing all over the place. I remarked that it looked as though we were really in for some sport; it didn't seem as if we could miss. While rigging up, I tried to make out what insects the fish were feeding on, and inasmuch as there were no flies to be seen, waited until I was set; still not seeing anything, I suggested to Bill that we had better put on nothing larger than a No. 16. Like most fishermen, I hate to go to the smaller flies unless absolutely necessary.

When we could not get a refusal from even one of the smaller fish that were rising, I decided it was time to find out just what the fish were taking, for we could see nothing from just casual observation. It didn't take long to see they were taking tiny flying ants. I told Bill we would have to get down to at least 20's, which was as small as I carried, for this was one of those rare years when we had a bit of summer fishing, due to cool weather and better-than-normal water.

But they ignored the 20's as they had everything else, and at that point neither of us had been able to raise a fish. I kept monkeying around with my flies and finally cut almost all the hackle off a little Dun Variant. Even that failed to get a fish up.

Finally I said to Bill, "To hell with this pool stuff. I'm going down below in the fast water to try to get some of my self-respect back." My ego was hurting, for never before had I seen so many fish working without being able to raise one. When I worked back up to him at almost dark, the trout were still showing all over the place and he still had not been able to raise a fish.

When we got home, I got right to work and wrote Ernie Schwiebert, author of that fine book *Matching the Hatch,* telling him my experience and asking him to come to my rescue. Because it may be of help to others, as it was to me, I quote part of his reply:

"The best terrestrial patterns for smutting feeders have been the black Jassids, beetles, and ants. The wings are lacquered and set in cement, and the winged patterns have their hackle trimmed out both top and bottom for a flat riding float. The ant relies as much on its dubbing as its hackle for an in-surface float. Sizes are 16 through 24; have sent larger ones so you can see how they are properly constructed. The tippets are decreased in size as hook sizes are decreased, for proper presentation. The platyl is .0059, and .0047 is excellent, and the Ulite Racine nylon from Rockland Tackle in Suffern is best in .0039 and .0031. These small sizes test at one pound and one-half pound; gentle strikes can set these little hooks, and then the playing is not difficult. These little tippets are surprisingly strong after the barb is set."

All I can say is that it takes a heck of a lot better fisherman than I am to fish that kind of tackle!

18

PATTERNS OLD AND NEW

THERE ARE MANY old and reliable patterns of dry flies that have not been mentioned in this book. They have not been left out because I think they are not good flies, but because they did not happen to fit into these pages.

Probably the most famous that has not been touched upon is that well-known fly the Fan-Wing Royal Coachman.

I doubt if there is any question that I am asked as often as this: "If your theory is correct, just what insect does the Fan-Wing Royal Coachman represent?"

First off, let me say that I have no *theories* on trout fishing. I gave up being a theorist some years ago, and for a very good reason. Invariably, just about the time a series of events would take place that made me feel I at last had the right theory, something would happen that blew it into a cocked hat.

True, I have made some studies, and listed herein are the results of these studies. It is my belief that there is quite a difference between listing the results of studies combined with experiences and theories.

Getting back to the Royal Coachman. They say confession is good for the soul, and I certainly must confess that I haven't the slightest idea what insect the Fan-Wing Royal is supposed to imitate.

Certainly no insect, aquatic or otherwise, has ever come to my attention that even closely approximates it. As a matter of fact, should I see such a creature flying about, I would probably think I had a touch of the sun "or else."

The obvious question, then, is why is this fly so successful and so widely used?

I believe its popularity is rather easy to understand, because it is doubtful if any pattern of trout fly, either dry or wet, has received as much publicity as the Fan-Wing Royal Coachman. Fishermen are normal human beings (although wives may think otherwise), and they respond to advertising, commercial or otherwise, the same as any other group. When they read on several occasions of fishermen making good catches on a certain fly, you can bet they are going to buy some to try them out. Very few flies have been mentioned as often as this one.

There are several things about this fly that make it appeal to both the fisherman and the fly-tyer.

The fisherman likes it because it floats pretty well, and it is a fly that he can *see*. And, too, it will of course catch him a few trout.

The fly-tyer likes it because it has been given a big build-up in every outdoor magazine in the country. It is shown on every color plate advertising flies that you can find, so that it is one fly that sells on sight as a rule. It is an inexpensive fly to tie, when compared to such flies as the Hendrickson or Quill Gordon, and the materials used in its construction are neither expensive nor difficult to obtain. The wing materials do not add greatly to the tyer's cost, being as a rule breast feathers from a mandarin or wood duck, and most commercial tyers buy the skins complete, having use for the flank feathers and wing feathers as well as the breast feathers.

In an honest effort, over a period of years, to determine what made the Fan Wing "click," I questioned every fisherman that I met about it.

Curiously enough, very few of the fishermen that I queried about it used the fly when there was a hatch on the water, for at such times all tried to imitate the fly that was emerging.

In all cases it was used instead for trying to "pound up" fish, and the fly seemingly did its best work in fast water, the heavier the better. In this kind of water trout do not have much time to look over a fly; it is a case of either take it or leave it.

If we fished the regular winged fly in such water it would be lost to us, whereas the Fan Wing shows up very plainly in almost any water where it can be kept above the surface.

This fly is also very popular for evening fishing, for the same reason. It can be seen when other flies cannot.

I have one big objection to all Fan-Wing flies. After catching a few fish on one, you might just as well throw it away, because unless you are extremely fortunate one of the wings will be "shot." There is just enough Scotch in me to make this go against the grain, and I have not used one in over five years. If a fly will not catch at least a couple of dozen trout before it becomes too battered for further use, I feel that I've been robbed. And it is always such a burden to put on another fly, at least it seems to be.

You can bet your last dollar that if there were not some other pattern of dry fly to take the place of the Fan Wing, with respect to its fish-taking ability, yours truly would use it, even if it were only good for one fish.

The Wulff-type fly has properly become popular—and for good reason. It floats well, will take a lot of abuse, and, most important, catches fish. The Royal Wulff in my opinion is far superior to the Royal Coachman and will of course stand up better. However, care must be exercised in fishing these flies. Watch your leader very carefully where the fly is attached. Due to their weight, they tend to fray 4X tippets rather fast.

Another popular dry fly that has not been mentioned is the Bivisible. They float well and are rather easy to follow on the water. On occasions they will take some good fish, but I do not believe they are as effective as the Fan-Wing fly.

Bivisibles are quite likely taken by trout for beetles or similar land insects that drop into the streams. A few years ago I did quite a bit of night fishing with a dry fly, and used a large Bivisible (brown) tied on a No. 8 hook, to fool trout that were feeding on June bugs that found their way to the pools. The stomach contents of fish caught showed that a number of these beetles had been taken, so it was a reasonable assumption that trout had taken the Bivisible, mistaking it for this insect. At any rate it took fish.

Of course, I have no way of proving this, and your guess on it is just as good as mine. One thing seems reasonably certain, though. It is to be doubted that a Bivisible would suggest a May fly to trout.

All in all, I do not believe that these flies are as consistently effective as other flies. Probably the best proof lies in the fact that nearly every fisherman encountered on the stream a few years ago had some Bivisibles, but of late years they seem to have lost most of their popularity.

These flies also go to pieces rather quickly, and more often than not, after a few fish are taken, a hackle will unwind, which means the beginning of the end for the fly.

To those of you who object to my running down your favorite patterns, and those who like to try something different, I would like to make a suggestion.

Forget your Fan Wings, Bivisibles, and the like for just a short time, and try instead all of the three following patterns: Grey Fox Variant, Dun Variant, Cream Variant.

You will note that the original purpose of this book is still being followed, i.e., to keep the number of patterns to a minimum. Each was mentioned previously in the correlating.

Variants, if tied with good hackles, will float better than any winged fly ever could, and they are easy to follow on the water. Owing to their construction, they descend very slowly to the water, and it is rarely that they cannot be seen at all times. On dark days when there is no sun, the Dun Variant is hard to find if it is once lost sight of when fishing fast water, and on such days I generally use the Grey Fox Variant, as it can be seen no matter how dull the day.

The Cream Variant does its best work, of course, in evening fishing, when most of the really light-colored flies are found on the stream.

If properly tied, one fly of this type will catch ten times as many fish, without going to pieces, so they have one big advantage over Fan Wings and Bivisibles, and on the whole I have found them much more effective.

To those of you who have never used this kind of fly, I wish to give one important bit of advice. A variant fly is only as good as the hackles with which it is tied. If the hackles are soft and full of web, leave the fly alone, for it would be money thrown away. A variant tied with soft, webby hackles will look more like a mop than a fly the minute it comes in contact with water, and its effectiveness is gone.

Very often the use of poor hackles is the reason these flies are tied on 16 and 18 hooks. They would not support a larger size. Personally, I like the large ones tied on either No. 10 or No. 12 hooks, depending on the length of the hackle filaments.

The fly-tyer from whom you purchase your flies may charge you slightly more per dozen for these flies, but if they are well tied they are worth the difference, and will save you money in the long run.

It has been my experience that the body materials used in variants are of little if any importance. I have tried tinsel, fur, and quills, and am partial to the latter, but not because they are any more effective with this type of body.

I have found that tinsel will not stay on a hook as long as either of the other two materials, and the fur will absorb a slight amount of water. The quill from a cock's hackle feather overcomes both of these disadvantages.

This type of fly rides high on the water, and fish see very little if any of the body, so for this reason it makes little difference about the material used in its construction.

When you are fishing variants, it will be noticed that on occasion the hackles will become messed up around the barb of the hook, and it pays to check on this every now and then, to make sure the hackles are as they should be.

In most cases, variants are tied with very short wings, but I cannot see where they are of any value to the fly. Why they are used, I do not know.

Some readers may think I've gone off the track, recommending flies that do not actually imitate natural insects. Such is not the case. Until the time comes when we definitely know exactly how things appear to trout, all we can do is pattern our flies so that they are suggestive of the fly life upon which they feed.

Roughly, natural May flies can be broken up into three color phases: the blue duns, the creams, and the grey and ginger combinations. Therefore, the Dun Variant is a variation of those flies tied to imitate the naturals that have blue dun wings, and the same is true with the Cream and Grey Fox Variants.

It is also suggested that no oily or greasy dressing be used on variants, or for that matter on any dry fly.

Actually, if the variant is well tied no floatant of any kind is necessary. If one is used, it should be something that will not mat the hackes together, for to do so reduces the effectiveness of the fly.

A solution I like is one that is very inexpensive and simple to make. It not only floats flies, but cleans them as well. It consists of carbon tetrachloride and Mucilin paste or any other good line dressing. Mix a piece of Mucilin about the size of a large bean with an ounce of the liquid. Carbon tetrachloride is a solvent, and dissolves the Mucilin in a few moments.

This liquid is very volatile, and even though the fly is soaked in it, it will be completely dry after two or three false casts are made, leaving a very light film of the floatant on the fly.

I like this better than any of the other homemade solutions consisting of ether, gasoline, or kerosene, because the danger of fire is eliminated. As carbon tetrachloride is used in extinguishing fires, it can be handled in safety—though its vapors are toxic—and being a cleaner, it does a lot to help keep flies in good order.

19

THE CARE OF DRY FLIES

MANY VALUABLE SUGGESTIONS on the care of fishing equipment, such as rods and lines, have been given in outdoor books and magazines, but for some unknown reason little space has ever been given to the proper care of dry flies.

Far too often, fishermen will be met on a stream, fishing with an expensive rod and reel, a good tapered line that fits the rod perfectly, and a properly tapered leader, all in good order. Then getting to the most important item of his whole equipment, from the standpoint of success or failure, we find a fly that was once a beautiful example of a fly-tyer's skill. Now, however, it looks like "two cents' worth of God help us."

It *must* be remembered that although the rod, reel, line, and leader combined may have cost a hundred dollars, and the fly cost only sixty-five cents tops, it is this low-cost item that we depend on to catch the fish.

There is no doubt about it, trout are getting more fussy all the time, owing to increased fishing pressure, and too much emphasis cannot be put on the importance of the appearance of the fly we are fishing with when using dry flies.

Unfortunately it is a fact that nine fishermen out of ten do not realize that the hackles on a dry fly are the determining factors in making it appeal to trout.

It makes no difference how well the fly was tied, or how good the quality of the hackles that were used in tying; if they are crushed and matted, the fly has lost 90 percent of its effectiveness.

I cannot recall ever having been advised about this little detail in the care of dry flies by anyone who sold me flies before I started making my own flies.

It is certainly to the fly-tyer's advantage to advise his customers on this point, for the more successful a fly is in taking fish, the more repeat business the tyer gets. Possibly some people think that everyone knows this, but I can prove that the opposite is the case.

Watch fishermen who are in their fishing out-fits buy flies. Eight out of ten of them will pick up flies that the tyer has used great pains in making and jam them into their fly boxes, which are already stuffed with flies. More likely than not, the box is not half deep enough to start with.

A fly left in such condition for a few hours will no more resemble its original appearance than a butterfly resembles a caterpillar.

It is just about as painful for a fussy fly-tyer to witness such a performance as it would be to see his best rooster killed. Obviously, the fisher-man does not realize what he is doing, because he would not lay down his hard-earned cash for a fly and then deliberately spoil it.

Up to a few years ago, the only fly box I was able to find that was deep enough to properly take care of dry flies with long hackles, such as vari-ants, was one made in England. It was aluminum, with separate compartments, each with a snap fastener, but it was so big and bulky that it was not practical to carry.

Then along came the Pyra-shell boxes, one type of which was one and a half inches deep and would care for most flies nicely. This box was still large but a big improvement over the others, for it was much lighter and less bulky, being less than half the size.

Next came the rotary-type box, which I have found very practical. It will take care of most winged flies and some of the smaller variants.

Someday I hope to be able to convince the manufacturers of this fly box that they should add just one-half inch to the depth of the box. It would then be an ideal carrier for all dry flies, as it would be two inches deep.

It hardly seems necessary to add another word of caution about not squeezing too many flies into a small receptacle. If fishermen will remember that the position of hackles on flies when purchased is the way they should be when placed on the water, it will be well worth their while.

Be sure a fly is thoroughly dry before putting it into a fly box. When fishing, and you want to change from one fly to another, make a few false casts with the fly to dry it thoroughly, remove the leader from the eye of the hook, straighten any hackles that might be curled, and put it away. Then when you want to use it again at some future time, it will be in good condition and ready for use—provided, of course, it has not been crushed in your box.

It is not advisable to stick dry flies in the fur, rubber, or cork bands sold for the purpose. These articles are excellent for nymphs, wet flies, and streamers, but it has been my experience that dry flies put in them mean curled hackles.

To recondition dry flies that have become "messed up," I have found nothing better than steam. If the hackles are of good quality and not too badly crushed, an application of steam will generally restore them to their original good condition. After doing this, be sure to set the fly aside for a few minutes before replacing in your fly box, to make sure that it is thoroughly dry.

To store dry flies from one season to the next, I first steam them and then stand them on their "noses," tails pointing upward. When put away in this manner neither the hackles nor the tails will curl, and they will be in good condition the following season.

If flies are to be stored over the summer months be sure to protect them with either camphor or paradichlorbenzene. Otherwise the larvae of either moths or Buffalo beetles or some other pest will make short work of them.

20

MATERIALS FOR ARTIFICIALS

IT WILL BE noted that the only materials listed in this book for making the bodies of flies are furs of various kinds, peacock quills, and quills from cocks' hackles.

Probably the poorest material that could be used is one found most commonly in commercially sold dry flies. This, of course, is wool.

The best argument against its use is the fact that wool absorbs water like a sponge. Certainly there is not much point in buying a fly constructed with a material that will tend to submerge it, when the object of the fly is to float as well as possible.

I recall some years ago one of the local farm boys who was an amateur fly-tyer came to me all elated. He had found the finest material for making bodies for Light Cahills that he ever saw. Not only was it easy to get, but it was just the right color, and was perfect in every way.

Admittedly, the samples he had looked good, and in response to my query as to what it was made of, he told me he had just pulled a bit of the light wool of the sheepskin from his coat.

When I asked him if he ever saw a sheep swim, he replied that it couldn't, because its wool would take up so much water it would be impossible for it to keep afloat.

He caught on quickly, and decided that he had a good body for wets, but not so hot for dries.

Wool is less translucent when wet than are the belly furs of fox or marten, and translucency is highly desirable in a dry fly.

In almost all cases where wool is used for bodies of dry flies it is dyed, and dyed materials should be avoided whenever possible.

The reason this material is used so extensively by fly-tyers is because it is easier for them in every way. Blending furs to get desired shades is not a simple task and takes quite a bit of time. It is much easier to work with a skein of dyed wool, and cheaper too. It is also a more lengthy job to spin a body with fur than with wool.

Any good fly-tyer will, if you request him to, make your flies with fur, if he is in the habit of using wool. Do not think he is being unfair when he charges you a few cents more a dozen for the flies. His cost is greater, and more time is required to make them.

It will be worth the slight difference in cost to you, for your fly will float better and be improved generally. Flies are the least expensive of any item of your equipment, yet they are the most important. Bear it in mind always.

Most fishermen who tie flies just for their own use seem to have a great deal of difficulty in removing the herl from the quills of peacock eyes.

Some writers on the subject recommend the use of a razor blade, and others soak the quills in water and remove the herl by rubbing an eraser along both sides of the quill. The latter way does a neat job, and none of the quill is lost.

After the herl is removed, the quills can be bleached by soaking them in peroxide overnight.

There is still another way that I stumbled on, and although considerably more expensive, it does a faster and better job. Those of you who have done this tedious work will probably be surprised when I say that an entire eye can be cleaned and bleached in less than two minutes. This is done with an ordinary household product that is found in most homes, and the name is Clorox.

This chemical removes the herl and bleaches in one quick operation, but being very powerful, it will sometimes ruin an entire peacock eye, making it too brittle to use.

However, I would far rather ruin a couple

of peacock eyes, which are comparatively inexpensive, than mess around cleaning the quills by the other methods. The time saved is well worth the cost of spoiling one peacock eye.

If you would care to experiment with this method, proceed as follows:

Immerse the complete eye in a small saucer filled with Clorox, making sure the feather is covered. Allow it to remain in the liquid until the herl disintegrates, leaving the quill bare. This usually takes less than a minute. Immediately when the quill seems free of herl, remove the eye and place it in a bowl containing water in which has been dissolved a tablespoonful of baking soda. This stops the action of the chemical. Then rinse in clear cold water.

If the eye is left in the first solution too long it will become too brittle, and you will be unable to wind it on a hook. After a bit of experimenting the proper time of immersion can be determined, and there will be very little loss.

Quills bleached in this manner are much lighter in color than any I have seen. They make beautiful bodies for Quill Gordons, because the dark stripe is not affected in any way, and it makes an excellent contrast. Be sure they are well soaked before tying.

If my suggestion is followed in using fine gold wire for ribbing the bodies of Quill Gordons, and the quills have been bleached in the above manner, the gold should be wound over the *darker* part of the quill.

Caution—Clorox is a powerful bleach, and care should be used that it is not spilled on any item of clothing. The manufacturer cautions that it should not be used on silk or wool.

The dressings of the first three dry flies mentioned in this book call for natural dun hackles, all being the same in that respect.

Too much stress cannot be put on the fact that natural dun hackles are far superior to those that have been dyed a dun color.

It is unfortunate for fishermen that the supply of these hackles is so limited. Were they available, there would of course be no necessity for dyeing white hackles to try to imitate the natural dun color, a characteristic color of the wings of so many May flies. There is no comparison between the natural and the dyed, although most fly-tyers hate to admit it.

Some writers recommend rusty dun hackles for some flies, medium duns for others, and dark duns for still others. As nearly as I have been able to determine, the exact shade of dun is of little consequence. It has been my experience that in imitating any fly that has a true blue-dun-colored wing, the exact shade of dun hackle used is relatively unimportant.

In checking over hundreds of specimens of the naturals, I have found there is a great deal of variation in the shade of the wings. Those on some flies of a species are much darker than the wings of others of the same species.

With this difference in shades occurring in the naturals, there seems to be little need to worry about the slight variation of color in the hackles of the artificial. I have found that for all practical purposes, a dun hackle of medium shade works equally well for Quill Gordon, Hendrickson, and Red Quill.

Most fishermen find it difficult to understand just why it is so hard to obtain flies tied with natural dun hackles, and why, if they can get them, they are forced to pay so much more for them.

To my knowledge, there is only one breed of chicken that closely resembles the birds from which we get our dun hackles. They are a breed known as Blue Andalusian, but unfortunately the hackles from them are of poor quality, and usually unsuited for good dry flies.

With such breeds as Leghorns, Plymouth Rocks, and Rhode Island Reds, the strain can be perpetuated by crossing a hen and cock of the same breed. This is not true with those birds from which we get our dun hackles.

The dun bird comes generally from crossing a white rooster with a black hen, or vice versa, and by doing so, if you are lucky, you may get a dun-colored chick.

Strangely enough, when you cross a dun-colored rooster with a hen of the same color, the chicks that hatch will be varied in color. There will be some white, some black, some black and white, some badger, and the rest dun, but as a rule very few of the latter. Because the strain is so very recessive, the chicks will usually revert to the original colors, black and white.

There is another peculiar thing about these birds. The largest proportion of chicks that are dun-colored will be hens, and it is not much trouble getting them, but good dun cocks are mighty valuable birds.

To illustrate what an uncertain proposition you are up against in trying to breed these birds, here is the luck I had last year. I set sixty eggs in an incubator. They had all been laid by dun hens crossed with dun roosters, both hens and cocks being the shade of dun I am always trying for.

Forty-eight chicks hatched, and seven showed definite traces of blue. However, when they started to get their adult plumage, I found I had one fair dun cock, another that was not worth raising, and three dun pullets. The others that showed some signs of being duns developed into badgers. Nice percentage, one out of sixty.

Everyone who has tried to raise these birds has noted another strange thing. The birds that are dun-colored as chicks are the weakest birds, and the most apt to die.

And of course if rats or weasels or other vermin happen to get at your chicks, it is always the blues that are taken.

Compared to other shades, dun hackles always seem to be of inferior quality, and seldom become prime on a rooster before he is two years old.

So you see, if you are fortunate enough to know where flies can be obtained with these hackles, you should not be surprised if your orders cannot always be filled. And, too, there is a mighty good reason for the slightly higher cost. The fly-tyer, who uses the naturals could buy dyed hackles at less expense to himself than it costs him to breed his dun birds, but raise them he must, for all the shops in the East could not get sufficient dun hackles to supply three fly-tyers who had any amount of business.

The only fly-tyer I know of who ties flies with natural dun hackles is Harry Darbee of Roscoe, New York.

AFTERWORD

IN CHECKING BACK, it will be found that only ten patterns of dry flies have been used in correlating the May flies and the artificials that represent them.

It is hoped that nobody will think I have implied that these are the only May flies upon which trout feed, for such is far from the truth.

They are, however, those of the most importance to fishermen, as are their imitations. By adding to this group a dry fly tied on a No. 18 hook, to imitate the very small May flies, I have found that for all practical purposes no other patterns are necessary. With these artificials, when well tied and properly presented, good fishing can be had throughout the entire season when trout are at all interested in surface food.

It is quite possible that on your favorite stream one or two of the May flies listed do not appear, and if such is the case, your assortment can be still further reduced. If you carried half a dozen of each pattern, the chances are you would have fewer flies in your collection than most fishermen generally "tote" with them.

Regardless of how well a fly is tied, or how nearly it matches the fly on the water, presentation is by far the most important factor, except in extreme cases. As a rule, a dry fly that is not offered in a lifelike manner will be passed up by larger trout.

Very often when there are no May flies on the water those trout not hiding are in such positions that they can watch the surface of the stream. If the water temperature is not too high, they will usually rise to any kind of insect floating into their line of vision. Such insects as flying ants, beetles, crickets, and grasshoppers are relished by trout. When they are feeding in this manner they are not so apt to be selective as when feeding on a hatch.

At such times they can be tempted to take a dry fly as long as care is used in approach and presentation. It must be remembered, too, that the fact that no fish can be seen feeding does not mean they would not feed if food were available.

When it seems no fish are moving, I am especially partial to a variant-type fly. There is someing about flies tied this way that seems to excite trout, and often they will come up and smash them when they do not want them. Every time this happens, it means another fish located, to try for at some other occasion. Very often it has been my good fortune to locate some really good fish in this manner that had not been raised by a fisherman right ahead of me.

Often fish that have "splashed" at a variant can be taken on a very small winged fly, after they have been rested for a few minutes. This is a good plan to remember at all times, and the same is true if the fish has raised to a small fly without taking it. Give him a ten-minute rest, and try for him with a variant. It will not work all the time, but often enough to make it worth trying.

Through this book, it will be noted that I have tried as much as possible to avoid the use of *positive* statements. But there is one statement I am safe in making, without fear of contradiction from any source: *It most certainly is worth any fisherman's while to study the fly life on every stream he fishes*. I make this assertion without reservation, and can promise any time spent in this manner will pay good dividends.

If a fishing contest were held between an average dry-fly fisherman who knew a stream from

A to Z and a person who never had done any fishing but was the world champion fly caster, which of the two would you put your money on?

Most of us would favor the man who knew the stream where the contest was to be held, even though he could not handle his tackle so well.

Every minute spent in studying fly life is time spent in finding out more about the stream. It is impossible to study the insect life in the streams we fish without at the same time making observations that are bound to help us to be more successful fishermen. Many of the things we will learn are closely related to the knowledge we must attain before we can become proficient in taking fish.

Trout are dependent to a great extent on the May-fly life in the streams. They seem to know where flies are going to emerge, and when. If the flies are a species that emerge in the riffles, the trout will feed on them there. The same is true with those flies whose nymphs spend all of their time in the still waters, and when the flies emerge there the fish will take them there.

A perfect example of this is the occurrence in the chapter on March Browns. Fish were feeding in an unusual part of the stream, but there was a good reason for it. They were there to take advantage of available food.

It follows, therefore, that the more a fisherman can learn about the food and feeding habits of trout, the better able he will be to meet conditions that arise when fishing.

This is not only true of fishing, as it is just as applicable to hunting.

The grouse hunter who knows what food the birds are feeding on, and also knows where the feeding areas are, is more apt to get some shooting than the chap who knows nothing about the birds, and who "just goes hunting." In time he will probably stumble on some birds, but he will more than likely lose a great deal of precious hunting time before he gets that break.

Whether or not you follow the suggestions given as to copying the naturals with specific imitations is not as important as the knowledge you will gain by learning to identify the insects and finding out about their habits.

Some readers may feel they get so darn little time to fish, they are not going to waste a lot of time messing around with a lot of bugs. True, fishing time may be limited, but unless the streams you fish are a lot different from any it has been my good fortune to fish on, there are always some periods during the day when there is little if any activity.

Yes, brother anglers, we have all seen those moments, and unfortunately there are too many of them. It is at such times that we can do a bit of studying, and I have yet to see a person who got started on it who did not get a real "bang" out of it. It is the most natural thing in the world to get a kick out of seeing some hitherto unexplained secret of Mother Nature unfold before our eyes.

Try it sometime, and unless I am greatly mistaken, it will add greatly to your fishing pleasure.

When there is a hatch of flies on the stream and fish are feeding on them, it seems a shame to take a minute off to catch one of the May flies, so as to identify it and to learn what artificial to put on. *Sure it does,* but it takes a darn sight longer to try three or four different flies before finding one you can take fish on.

I have not gone into fishing technique or fly-tying. These two subjects are covered in a much more able manner than I could in books that are already available to fishermen.

Here's hoping that by the end of next season, when some stranger meets you on the stream and, after admiring a few good browns and rainbows in your creel, asks what fly you caught them on, you will be able to reply proudly by giving him the name of the artificial as well as the proper name of the natural. May all your troubles be little ones, and all your trout big ones.

NATURAL AND ARTIFICIAL FLIES

Natural and Artificial	Description of Natural *	Dry-Fly Imitation	Normal Emergence Time	Nymph Imitation	Hook Size
Iron fraudator (Quill Gordon)	Wings, dun color; two tails; faint brown markings on legs. Female slightly larger and lighter in color than male. Size from head to end of tail, approx. 13/16 inch.	Quill Gordon	1:30 P.M. E.S.T.	Quill Gordon tied wet	12 or 14
Ephemerella subvaria (Hendrickson and Red Quill)	Wings, dun color; three tails, speckled. Bodies of females have dark pinkish cast. Males a more reddish cast. Bodies are a bit heavier than those of Quill Gordon. Size from head to end of tail, approx. 7⁄8 inch.	M., Red Quill F., Hendrickson	2:00 P.M. E.S.T.	Hendrickson	12 or 14 12
	Blasturus cupidas often emerges at same time as *E. subvaria*. Looks similar to male *E. subvaria* except center tail is shorter than other two tails and body is darker.	Red Quill	2:00 P.M. E.S.T.		12

Species	Description	Imitation	Hatch	Fly	Hook
Stenonema vicarium (March Brown)	First of the large flies to appear. Wings slant back more than on other flies and are mottled brown. Bodies on underside are buff colored. Brown segments on upper part of body. Two tails, mottled. Brown markings on legs. Size from head to end of tails, approx. 1 to 1⅛ inches. Males smaller.	American March Brown	sporadic, usually starts about 10:00 A.M. E.S.T.	March Brown	10 or 12
Stenonema fuscum (Grey Fox)	A light counterpart of March Brown; very similar, except slightly smaller and lighter in color. Appears yellow in the air or on the water in sunlight. Wings faintly mottled; legs have distinct brown markings. Size from head to end of tails, approx. 1 inch. Males smaller.	Grey Fox	same as above	same as above	12
Stenonema canadensis and *ithaca* (Light Cahill)	Same general characteristics as above, but smaller and more yellowish cast to wings. Has smaller eyes. From head to end of tails, approx. ⅞ inch. Males smaller.	Light Cahill	sporadic; usually later than Grey Fox	same as above	12 or 14

Paraleptophlebia adoptiva, etc. (May-Fly Midgets)	Very small, dark dun-colored flies. Their small size is their identifying characteristic.	very small dark Dun Variant	about 11:00 A.M. E.S.T.		18 or 20
Ephemera guttulata (Green Drake)	Largest of the stream May flies. Wings have greenish cast. Underside of bodies almost white, dark stripes full length of upper part. Three tails. Size from head to end of tails, 1½ inches. Males much smaller than females.	large Grey Fox Variant	sporadic		10 or 12 short shank
Isonychia bicolor (Dun Variant)	Wings, very dark dun. Body reddish-brown. Forelegs brown; middle and hind legs yellow. Size from head to end of tails, approx. 1⅛ inches.	large dark Dun Variant	evening (see text for exception)	Isonychia nymph	10 or 12 short shank nymph 10 regular
Potamanthus distinctus (Cream Variant)	Wings and underside of body, very light cream. Size from head to end of tails, approx. 1 inch.	Cream Variant	evening		12 short shank

Ephemerella attenuata (Blue-winged Olive)	Wings, very dark dun color; three tails, body of newly emerging fly olive, darkening as fly is exposed to the air.	Small Dun Variant with olive body	starting 9:00 A.M. E.S.T.	Blue-winged Olive, wet	16 or 18

* The sizes of the naturals vary in different streams. For example, in the Schoharie, a fairly large stream, flies will be considerably larger than the same species in the Eastkill, or Westkill, tributaries of the Schoharie. It follows, then, that hook sizes should be smaller for flies used on smaller streams.

173

DATE	RIVER, WATER TEMPERATURE, AND OTHER STREAM INFORMATION	FLY	TIME
STREAMSIDE EMERGENCE RECORDS